8.95

by COLIN STEWART EXTRA MASTER MARINER

revised by JOHN S. STYRING

ADLARD COLES LTD

in association with
RUPERT HART-DAVIS LTD
36 Soho Square, London W1
JOHN DE GRAFF Inc., New York

FLAGS, FUNNELS & HULL COLOURS

First published 1953
5th Impression (Revised) October 1959
New Edition—Revised and Enlarged—April 1963
Copyright in all countries
Signatory to the Berne Convention

PUBLISHERS' NOTE

THIS entirely new and enlarged edition of FLAGS, FUNNELS AND HULL COLOURS is the successor to Captain Colin Stewart's smaller book of which five impressions were required. The increase in the number of *House Flags and Funnels*, to well over twice the number in the original book, placed some limitation upon the hull colour feature of this new edition. However, a reasonable representation of the hull features of the leading shipping companies has been achieved by the introduction of a separate section. The section on Merchant Flags has also been enlarged.

The publishers are grateful to Mr John S. Styring, the well-known consultant on Merchant Marine flags and funnels, who has been responsible for the new information needed to enlarge this edition. From his unique collection of about 25,000 flags and funnels, some of which go back for over a century, he has selected over 1,000 as representative of the world's shipping companies today.

The author is personally grateful to Mr Laurence Dunn for permitting unrestricted use of his records for the revision of the *Hull Colour* section.

© Adlard Coles Ltd. 1963
Printed in Great Britain by
W. & J. Mackay & Co. Ltd., Chatham

CONTENTS

INTRODUCTION

MANY shipping companies have come and gone and they will continue to do so; perhaps that is one of the features which make the subject of flags, funnels and hull colours so interesting, but it also makes the problem of giving a balanced and reasonable representation of world shipping just as difficult as ever. Fortunately with the increase in the number of entries in this edition it has been possible to give a wider general coverage and to include many little known companies of the smaller nations of the world.

Although the identification of funnel markings or hull colours of the large well-known shipping companies can on occasion provide some difficulty, that of the smaller or subsidiary companies is often even more problematical. For instance, a ship owned by one company but managed by another may well be in the colours of the managing firm (or charter company) and not have her hull and funnel painted in the colours of her owner. Indeed it has not been unknown for a combination of each company's colours to be seen together!

Also worth noting is the fact that some companies have different funnel and/or hull colours for different types of ships. For example F. T. Everard and Son Ltd. sometimes favour a buff or yellow funnel and hull for their motor vessels but black funnels and hulls for their older vessels; the P and O also have dual colours, with buff funnels and white hulls for their larger passenger liners and black for both features of their cargo ships and tankers. Another recent feature of interest is afforded by the "Shell" company. Their new giant tankers have their hulls painted green, whilst their twin (side by side) funnels become an assistance to identification, although this feature is not unique to the company.

In this book it has been necessary to illustrate a "standard" type of modern funnel which is so proportioned that the colour features on it may be reasonably shown. However it must be remembered that many modern funnels are either so squat or so narrow, with "styled" streamlining, that the original balance of the funnel marking against the basic overall funnel colour can be greatly upset. Sometimes the styling is such that from a distance only the top of the funnel with a predominating colour band will show. Further, the bands, stripes or other features may themselves be "stylized", and thus appear somewhat different from those shown in these pages.

A glance through the coloured plates will show many features of interest. For instance many a funnel has the owning company's flag on it, but only one flag is known to portray a funnel. Also to be seen are many flags and funnels of very similar, if not of always identical, design.

The logical step from identifying the company to which a ship belongs by her funnel markings and house flag, is to identify the ship herself—or at least her type. This is not nearly so difficult as some believe and the art is well explained in Laurence Dunn's book *Ship Recognition—Merchant Ships*. As any sailor knows, a ship has a definite character, each ship being different in some way even to her sister, and to an observer ashore or afloat there is the greatest satisfaction to be gained from correctly answering the question "What ship is that?"

HOUSE FLAGS AND THEIR ORIGINS

It is usual, customary and correct for the house flag of a company to be worn at the mainmast head; however there are exceptions, and, as Commander Hilary Mead has pointed out in his book on Sea Flags,* the Brocklebank Line have always used the foremast. Today with many single-masted ships it can only be worn at the fore, although the author has seen it on a starboard yard when the foremast head has been taken by a complimentary ensign, and also on a stumpy bridge-mast when the other masts have been lowered for docking purposes.

The story of the design of each flag would make interesting reading, especially of the older companies. Many, however, are self-evident by the use of the alphabetical initials of the company upon plain coloured flags; though even these show subtleties of design. An example of this is that of the Lamport and Holt Line, who do not have an "&" between the letters "L" and "H"; but a +. This is more symbolic of the personality of the line founded, in the nineteenth century, by W. J. Lamport and George Holt.

The national "character" of a company can often be seen in its house flag; for instance the Irish Shipping Company's house flag has the red diagonal cross of St. Patrick with the addition of the arms of the four Provinces, one in each division of the field.

For beauty in design, so often lost these days in the desire to advertise a product on a house flag, the Stag Line is difficult to surpass. This company's flag (and funnel)

*Sea Flags—Their General Use, Brown, Son & Ferguson Ltd., Glasgow.

bear the crest of the Robinson family, who founded the firm in 1846.

The truth of the origins of many house flags has sometimes been disputed and the stories regarded as sailors' yarns, but many of the explanations are given "officially" by the companies—and, after all, the stories of tramps and sailors usually have a measure of truth.

The origin of the house flag of the Federal Steam Navigation Company is of considerable interest. In 1824 the *Sir Edward Pagel*, one of Money Wigram's clippers, was anchored off Spithead wearing the St. George's cross at the main. That was and still is, the flag flown by an Admiral and so a naval pinnace was sent by an H.M. frigate to investigate. There being no Admiral aboard, the Master was censured and ordered to haul down the flag, but thinking his masthead looked bare he re-hoisted the flag after a blue pocket handkerchief had been sewn in the middle of the cross.

A further interesting flag is that of the P and O (Peninsular and Oriental) Steam Navigation Company. In the Portuguese Insurrection of 1832, Wilcox and Anderson, London shipowners, rendered valuable service to Queen Maria, providing ships and ammunition and helping to raise a loan in England, all at considerable financial and personal risk to the partners. Similarly, in the Carlist Insurrection in Spain, the two gave active support to the cause of Isabella, the Queen Regent. Both by Portugal and Spain these services were rewarded with valuable trading facilities, and the flag of the partners—later the P and O—commemorates this early history, the blue and white being

5

the national colours of Portugal quartered with the red and yellow of Spain.

Sometimes a flag and a pennant are worn together, and quoting Boyd Cable, Commander Hilary Mead points out that this combination has its origin in the days of the sail era. When steam propulsion was first introduced it was not always possible to distinguish a steam from a sailing vessel because the funnel may well have been hidden by masts. To facilitate this distinction a pennant known as a "steam cornet" was hoisted in addition to the house flag. The custom survives today. In fact the burgee worn by Trinity House ships is still termed a cornet.

The origin of this double signification is undoubtedly true, but the amalgamation of two companies would also give cause for this, as with the Moss Hutchison Line. Their fleet which runs to the Iberian peninsula wear both the old Moss Line pennant, and the tri-colour of the old J. and P. Hutchison company; their Mediterranean fleet wearing only the pennant.

The ships of the Glen Line, in which are inaugurated those of the Shire Line, wear the Glen Line house flag. The blue pennant with the white Maltese Cross being worn, according to the Company's tradition, to commemorate the Glen Line victories in the China Tea Race in 1874. Their ship the *Glenartney* gained this "blue riband" with a passage time from Woosung to London in 44 days.

It is also of interest to note that each vessel of the Clan Line carries a flag on the jackstaff, at the bow of the ship, which is that of the tartan of the Clan after which the ship is named. Upon the tartan background is also the lion of the house flag.

Ships of the Clan Line—as well as those of associated companies such as the Union Castle Line—may also be seen wearing the British and Commonwealth Shipping Company's swallow-tailed burgee superior to their own, as this company controls the group.

Many other interesting facts could be brought to light, but space does not permit. The changes of design of the Orient Line house flag here illustrated, show quite clearly the origin of their house flag today—the *blue colour* of the St. George's Cross being the only remaining similarity to the original house flag of Anderson Thomson and Co.

WORLD TOTAL TONNAGES (see page 68 for national tonnages)

For 1962 *Lloyd's Register of Shipping* gave the total number of merchant ships in the world as 38,661 or more, representing 139,979,813 tons gross; of these 4,922 were oil tankers with a total gross tonnage of 45,303,702. Comparing today's world totals with those given ten years ago when this book was first published, there has been an increase of about 7,000 ships of some 48 million tons gross; although the total figures include ships laid up or on the "reserve".

THE HOUSE FLAG OF THE BRITISH AND COMMONWEALTH SHIPPING COMPANY

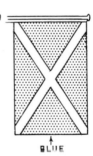

DEVELOPMENT OF A HOUSE FLAG

1. House flag of Anderson, Anderson & Co., formerly Anderson, Thomson & Co., flown by their Orient line Clippers. 1877, first house flag flown by steamships in the joint Australian Service. Changed in 1878.

2. House flag of R. & H. Green & Co., which had become F. Green & Co., when the Company joined with Andersons to form the joint Australian Service.

3. 1878. Original Orient S.N. Co's house flag, a combination of the Anderson and the Green flags. Only flown until about 1880.

4. 1880 until about 1892. Similar to the Pacific Steam Navigation Co's house flag except for their lettering, "P.S.N.C."

5. About 1892 to 1908.

6. 1908 to present day. The letters were dropped on the Company becoming independent of the P.S.N.C. and R.M.S.P.Co. It is now the Orient Line house flag, which company has in recent years become part of the "P & O-Orient Lines".

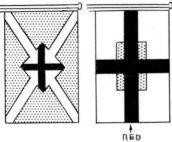

RED

BLUE

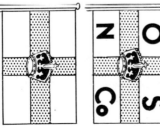

COLOURING AND FUNNEL SEQUENCE

WHEN using four-colour line blocks it is not always possible to obtain exact shades of colour; indeed shades of colour used on ships are often unique. However, the basic colours of red, blue and yellow together with black, grey, white and green are represented; and if a tone is most marked, e.g. a very light or dark blue, this has been shown. The yellow used for this printing is deep to obtain clarity, and is intended to indicate all its tones and shades as well as cream, buff and gold. The same yellow is combined with blue to obtain green, which again is a conventional green, to cover the many varying shades in use.

A letter "G" by a colour signifies that it is gold, in a similar manner an "S" or "Al" signifies silver or aluminium.

The order of presentation of the funnels has been difficult, owing to the wide range in combinations of colours and design. However, the following method has been adopted as being the most logical and practical:

1. Each basic funnel colour has been taken in turn in the following order: BLACK, GREY (or Silver or Aluminium), WHITE, YELLOW, BLUE, GREEN, ORANGE and RED. A funnel with a black (or coloured) top generally forms a variation of a basic colour.
2. The same colour order as above is retained for the order of the coloured horizontal stripes or bands.

3. A funnel with a *single* band—each possible colour being taken in turn—follows the funnels of all one colour and precedes those with double or triple bands. But *narrow* edging bands (or centre stripes) of different colour on the single band of predominating colour, is not considered to make the funnel multi-banded.
4. Bands adjacent to each other (i.e. touching) or colours in a miscellaneous pattern are usually grouped at the end of each basic funnel colour group.

In general the above order has been maintained but there is unavoidable ambiguity and occasionally the "rules" have been broken to facilitate identification. A close study of the colour pages will also reveal arrangements within arrangements; for instance letters on a funnel or band come before symbols (or devices), which in turn precede the use of a replica of the house flag as a funnel marking.

In common with most "arts", only experience and practice can bring perfection and the exceptions to the rules give additional interest to the subject. The black and white outlines of flags and funnels are provided to enable additional information to be recorded by the publisher (or reader) in future editions. This facility can be made use of in conjunction with the notes and corrigenda at the end of the book.

INTERNATIONAL CODE FLAGS

THE International Code Flags shown opposite are recognized by all countries and used for signalling between ships. If care is not taken it is possible when observing ships with unusual masts or rigging, to mistake a signal flag for a house flag.

Single code flags have a meaning of some urgency but they may be used in combination of two or more, when a code book is required to obtain their meaning. A ship on entering or leaving harbour may fly a four-lettered group of flags. This is the vessel's registration letters; for British vessels the four-lettered group commences with "G" or "M".

More details about sea signalling are given in the Bosun Book No. 8—*Sea Signalling Simplified* by Captain P. J. Russell.

INTERNATIONAL CODE FLAGS

SINGLE FLAG MEANINGS

A I am undergoing a speed trial.

B I am taking in or discharging explosives.

C Yes (affirmative).

D Keep clear of me—I am manoeuvring with difficulty.

E I am directing my course to starboard.

F* I am disabled. Communicate with me.

G I require a pilot.

H I have a pilot on board.

I I am directing my course to port.

J I am going to send a message by semaphore.

K* You should stop your vessel instantly.

L* You should stop. I have something important to communicate.

M I have a doctor on board.

N No (negative).

O* Man overboard.

P* *In harbour* (Blue Peter): All persons are to repair on board as the vessel is about to proceed to sea.

At sea: Your lights are out, or burning badly.

Q My vessel is healthy and I request a free pratique.

R* The way is off my ship; you may feel your way past me.

S My engines are going full speed astern.

T* Do not pass ahead of me.

V* I require assistance.

W* I require medical assistance.

X Stop carrying out your intentions and watch for my signals.

Y I am carrying mails.

Z* To be used to address or call shore stations.

Usually sent by flashing in morse code.

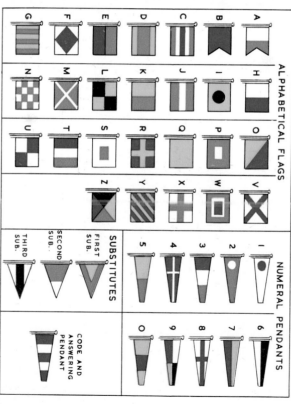

ALPHABETICAL FLAGS

NUMERAL PENDANTS

SUBSTITUTES — FIRST SUB., SECOND SUB., THIRD SUB.

CODE AND ANSWERING PENDANT

F.F.—B

9

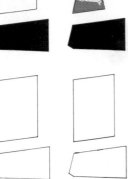

For Country of Ownership see p. 68, and for entries marked
† *see p. 88.*

1	Miyachi Kisen K.K.	Jp.
2	China Navigation Co. Ltd.	G.B.
3	A. Kirsten	Gm.(W)
4	Koninklijke Rotterdamsche Lloyd N.V.	Nd.
5	Worms et Cie.	Fr.
6	Cia Trasatlantica Espanola	Sp.
7	Soc. des Transports Maritimes Petroliers	Fr.
8	Clyde Shipping Co. Ltd.	G.B.
9	Bolton Steam Shipping Co. Ltd.	G.B.
10	China Pacific Navigation Co. Ltd.	G.B.
11	Cie. des Messageries Maritimes	Fr.
12	Soc. Maritime Nationale	Fr.
13	Citerna Maritime	Fr.
14	Sun Oil Co.	U.S.A.
15	Watts, Watts & Co. Ltd. (Britain S.S. Co. Ltd.)	G.B.
16	William Robertson, Shipowners, Ltd.	G.B.
17	P. Henderson & Co.	G.B.
18	Red Anchor Line Ltd.	G.B.
19	Anchor Line Ltd.	G.B.
20	Mollers' Ltd.	G.B.
21	Eastern & Australian Steamship Co. Ltd.	G.B.
22	Peninsular & Oriental Steam Navigation Co.	G.B.
23	Henry M. Thomson	G.B.
24	Cia Nacional de Navegação	Pg.
25	China Merchants Steam Navigation Co. Ltd.	Ci(H)
26	North Yorkshire Shipping Co. Ltd.	G.B.
27	Olaf Boe & Co.	Nr.
28	Soc. Nationale des Chemins de Fer Francais	Fr.
29	Cie de Navigation Denis Frères	Fr.
30	Hain Steamship Co. Ltd.	G.B.
31	Arnt J. Morland	Nr.
32	Maurel & Prom	Fr.
33	Patzlaff & Zuckschwerdt G.m.b.H.	Gm.(W)
34	W. Schuchmann	Gm.(W)
35	Transportes, Aduanas y Consignaciones S.A.	Sp.

1
to
35

1
to
35

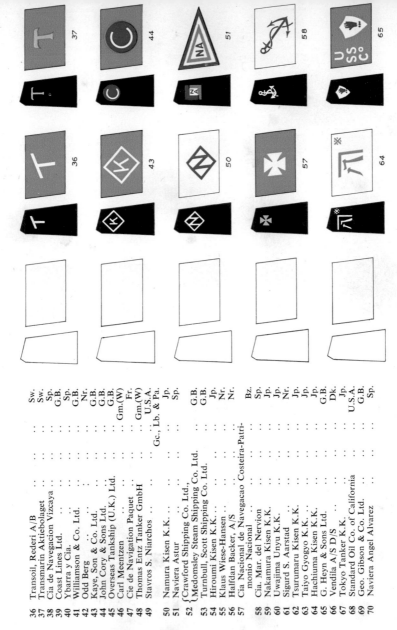

36	Transoil, Rederi A/B	Sw.
37	Transmarin Aktiebolaget	Sw.
38	Cia de Navegacion Vizcaya	Sp.
39	Coast Lines Ltd.	G.B.
40	Ybarra y Cia.	Sp.
41	Williamson & Co. Ltd.	G.B.
42	Odd Berg	Nr.
43	Kaye, Son & Co. Ltd.	G.B.
44	John Cory & Sons Ltd.	G.B.
45	Overseas Tankship (U.K.) Ltd.	G.B.
46	Carl Meentzen	Gm.(W)
47	Cie de Navigation Paquet	Fr.
48	Thomas Entz Tanker GmbH	Gm.(W)
49	Stavros S. Niarchos	U.S.A.
		Gc., Lb. & Pa.
50	Namura Kisen K.K.	Jp.
51	Naviera Astur	Sp.
52	{Crawford Shipping Co. Ltd., {Medomsley Steam Shipping Co. Ltd.	G.B.
53	Turnbull, Scott Shipping Co. Ltd.	G.B.
54	Hiroumi Kisen K.K.	Jp.
55	Klaus Wiese-Hansen	Nr.
56	Halfdan Backer, A/S	Nr.
57	Cia Nacional de Navegacao Costeira-Patri-monio Nacional	Bz.
58	Cia. Mar. del Nervion	Sp.
59	Nakamura Kisen K.K.	Jp.
60	Uwajima Unyu K.K.	Jp.
61	Sigurd S. Aarstad	Nr.
62	Tsurumaru Kisen K.K.	Jp.
63	Taiyo Gyogyo K.K.	Jp.
64	Hachiuma Kisen K.K.	Jp.
65	G. Heyn & Sons Ltd.	G.B.
66	Vendila A/S D/S	Dk.
67	Tokyo Tanker K.K.	Jp.
68	Standard Oil Co. of California	U.S.A.
69	Geo. Gibson & Co. Ltd.	G.B.
70	Naviera Angel Alvarez	Sp.

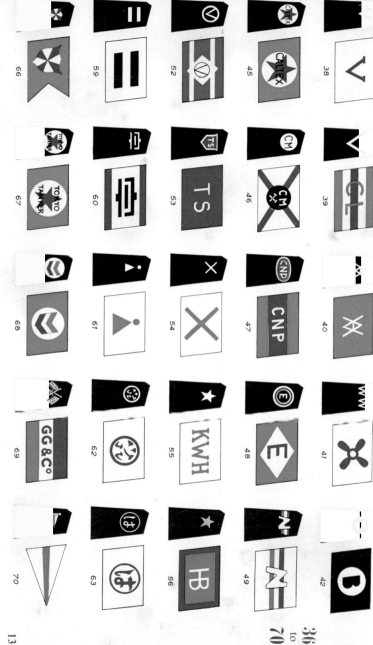

66

59

52

45

38   V

67   TOKYO TANKER

60

53   TS

46   CM

39   CL

68

61

54   X

47   CNP

40

69   GG & Cº

62

55   KWH

48   E

41

70

63

56   HB

49   N

42   B

71	Soc. Nationale d'Affretements	: :	Fr.
72	S. Ugelstad	: :	Nr.
73	Leonhardt & Blumberg	: :	Gm.(W)
74	Erhardt & Dekkers	: :	Nd.
75	Verenigde Tankkustvaart N.V.	: :	Nd.
76	Booth Steamship Co. Ltd.	: :	G.B.
77	Cie Nationale de Navigation	: :	Fr.
78	F. T. Everard & Sons Ltd.	: :	G.B.
79	Rafen & Loennechen	: :	Nr.
80	Koninklijke Java-China-Paketvaart Lijnen N.V.	: :	Nd.
81	American Trading & Production Corpn.	: :	U.S.A.
82	Clemente Campos y Cia.	: :	Sp.
83	General Steam Navigation Co. Ltd.	: :	G.B.
84	Donaldson Line Ltd.	: :	G.B.
85	Francesco Longobardo	: :	Iy.
86	Currie Line Ltd.	: :	G.B.
87	Colonial Sugar Refining Co. Ltd.	: :	G.B.
88	Bergh & Helland	: :	Nr.
89	Giuseppe Bozzo fu Lorenzo	: :	Iy.
90	Ambrosino Scotto Pugliese	: :	Fr.
91	Stephenson Clarke Ltd.	: :	G.B.
92	Pittaluga, Ditta Luigi, Vapori	: :	Iy.
93	Sicilarma Soc. di Nav.	: :	Iy.
94	Moss Hutchison Line Ltd.	: :	G.B.
95	J. & A. Gardner & Co. Ltd.	: :	G.B.
96	Rederi A/B Iris	: :	Sw.
97	Bugsier Reederei und Bergungs A. G.	: :	Gm.(W)
98	Hagb. Waage	: :	Nr.
99	William Sloan & Co. Ltd.	: :	G.B.
100	Meiji Kaiun K.K.	: :	Jp.
101	O. F. Ahlmark & Co. Eftr., A/B	: :	Sw.
102	Asahi Kisen K.K.	: :	Jp.
103	Surrendra (Overseas) Private Ltd.	: :	I.
104	A. Zedler	: :	Gm.(W)
105	{J. A. Billmeir & Co. Ltd., {Stanhope Steamship Co. Ltd.	: :	G.B.

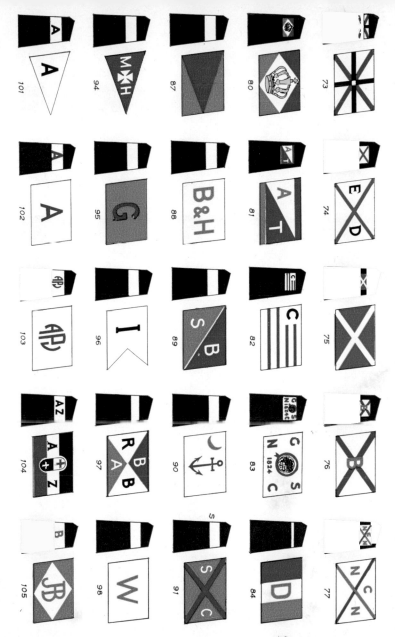

No.	Company	Country
106	Corrado, Soc di Navigazione	Iy.
107	Dani & C.	Iy.
108	John T. Essberger	Gm.(W)
109	Erling Hansen	Nr.
110	Ernst Russ	Gm.(W)
111	Wm. France, Fenwick & Co. Ltd.	G.B.
112	Carl Norrthon Jr.	Sw.
113	J. & C. Harrison Ltd.	G.B.
114	John S. Monks Ltd.	G.B.
115	Lundegaard & Sonner	Nr.
116	Metcalfe Shipping Co. Ltd.	G.B.
117	Cia. Maritima	Pp.
118	Auxiliar Maritima S.A.	Sp.
119	Nissho Kisen K.K.	Jp.
120	Purvis Shipping Co. Ltd.	G.B.
121	Parodi, Soc. per Azioni Emanuele V.	Iy.
122	Moor Line Ltd. (Walter Runciman & Co.)	G.B.
123	Renwick, Wilton & Dobson Ltd.	G.B.
124	Svea, Stockholms Rederi A/B	Sw.
125	Reederei Willy H. Schlieker & Co.	Gm.(W)
126	Trelleborgs Angfartygs A/B	Sw.
127	F. A. Vinnen & Co.	Gm.(W)
128	Cia Naviera Vascongada	Sp.
129	Tidewater Oil Co. Inc.	U.S.A.
130	A. R. Appelqvist A/B	Sw.
131	Aug. Bolten	Gm.(W)
132	Friedrich A. Detjen Reederei	Gm.(W)
133	Reederei Eugen Friederich	Gm.(W)
134	Odd Godager & Co.	Nr.
135	Jens Toft A/S (D/S Jutlandia A/S)	Dk.
136	Lykes Bros. Steamship Co. Inc.	U.S.A.
137	Malvicini, Soc. G. Officine Meccaniche Riparazione Nav-Vapori	Iy.
138	Pope & Talbot Inc.	U.S.A.
139	O. M. Thore	Sw.
140	Newbigin S.S. Co. Ltd.	G.B.

106 to 140

16

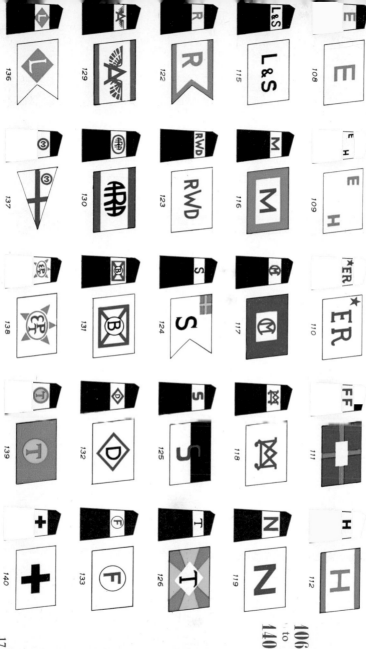

136

129

122

115

108

137

130

123

116

109

138

131

124

117

110

139

132

125

118

111

140

133

126

119

112

106
to
140

17

No.	Company	Country
141	Headlam & Son	G.B.
142	Sigval Bergesen	Nr.
143	Socony Mobil Oil Co. Inc.	U.S.A.
144	Lambert Bros. Ltd.	G.B.
145	Cia. Arrendataria del Monopolio de Petroleos S.A.	Sp.
146	Wm. Cory & Son Ltd.	G.B.
147	T. G. Irving Ltd.	G.B.
148	Angel Riva Suardiaz	Sp.
149	Marius Nielsen & Son	Dk.
150	Holm & Wonsild	Dk.
151	Charles Hill & Sons	G.B.
152	Hudig & Veder N.V.	Nd.
153	Knohr & Burchard	Gm.(W)
154	Ragnar Kallstrom	Sw.
155	Esso Petroleum Co. Ltd.	G.B.
156	Baltic Trading Co. Ltd.	G.B.
157	Mitsubishi Kaiun K.K.	Jp.
158	Nakano Kisen K.K.	Jp.
159	Sanko Kisen K.K.	Jp.
160	Hara Shosen K.K.	Jp.
161	Taiyo Kaiun Sangyo K.K.	Jp.
162	Shofuku Kisen K.K.	Jp.
163	Yamamoto Kisen K.K.	Jp.
164	Lubeck Linie A. G.	Gm.(W)
165	Kyoritsu Kisen K.K.	Jp.
166	Kyokuyo Hogei K.K.	Jp.
167	A. Yllera	Sp.
168	Glassel & Co.	Gm.(W)
169	Atlantic Refining Co.	U.S.A.
170	Jens Henriksen	Nr.
171	Ubaldo Gennari fu Torquato	Iy.
172	Emilio Canale di Pietro	Iy.
173	Raffaele Romano	Iy.
174	Rickmers Rhederei A. G.	Gm.(W)
175	Unterweser Reederei A. G.	Gm.(W)

141 to 175

18

141
to
175

19

No.	Company	Country
176	International Union Lines Ltd.	Lb.
177	J. A. Reinecke	Gm.(W)
178	Federico G. Fierro	Sp.
179	John Milligen & Co. Ltd.	G.B.
180	Johs. Fritzen & Sohn	Gm.(W)
181	Einar Lange	Nr.
182	Bergens Kulkompani A/S	Nr.
183	A/S Star Shipping	Nr.
184	Pocahontas S.S. Co.	U.S.A.
185	Charles le Borgne	Fr.
186	Olaf Pedersens Rederi A/S	Nr.
187	L. A. Jackson (Shipping) Ltd.	G.B.
188	Madison Shipping Corpn.	Lb.
189	Alfred C. Toepfer Schiffs.	Gm.(W)
190	Mullion & Co. Ltd.	G.B.
191	Bernuth, Lembcke Co. Inc.	U.S.A.
192	Buries, Markes Ltd.	G.B.
193	American Export Lines Inc.	U.S.A.
194	Herlof Andersens Rederi A/S	Nr.
195	Louis Dreyfus & Cie.	Fr.
196	Mayflower S.S. Corpn.	U.S.A.
197	Montship Lines Ltd.	G.B.
198	Rederi A/B Nordic	Sw.
199	Cie de Navigation Mixte	Fr.
200	Plouvier Maritime S.A.	Bl.
201	Sagland Ltd.	G.B.
202	Soc. Geral de Comercio, Industria e Transportes	Pg.
203	Torm Dampskibsselskabet A/S	Dk.
204	Erik Winther.	Dk.
205	Havenbedrijf Mabesoone N.V.	Bl.
206	Hansa, Deutsche Dampfs.	Gm.(W)
207	S. M. Kuhnle & Son	Nr.
208	Scheepvaart en Steenkolen Maatschappij N.V.	Nd.
209	Shipping & Coal Co. Ltd.	G.B.
210	Sigurd Bruusgaard	Nr.

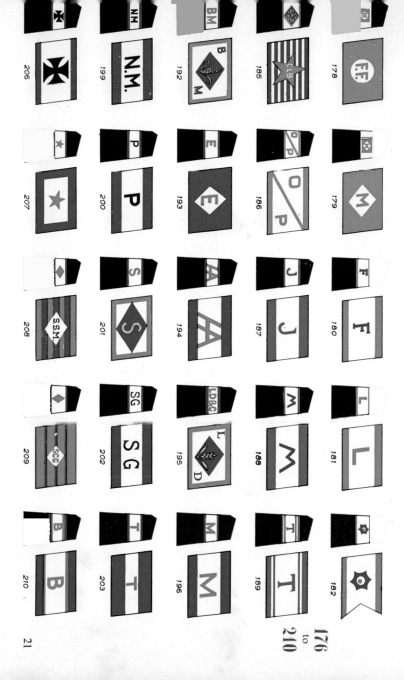

206 · 199 N.M. · 192 B M · 185 CLB · 178 F.F.

207 · 200 P · 193 E · 186 O P · 179 M

208 S.S.M. · 201 S · 194 A · 187 J · 180 F

209 SCC · 202 S G · 195 L D · 188 M · 181 L

210 B · 203 T · 196 M · 189 T · 182

176 to 210

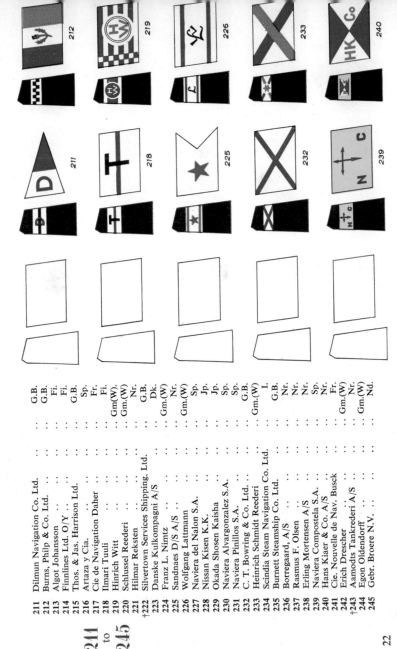

211	Dilmun Navigation Co. Ltd.	.. ..	G.B.
212	Burns, Philp & Co. Ltd.	.. ..	G.B.
213	Algot Johansson	.. ..	Fi.
214	Finnlines Ltd. O/Y ..	.. ..	Fi.
215	Thos. & Jas. Harrison Ltd.	..	G.B.
216	Artaza y Cia.	.. ..	Sp.
217	Cie de Navigation Daher	..	Fr.
218	Ilmari Tuuli	.. ..	Fi.
219	Hinrich Witt	.. ..	Gm(W).
220	Schlussel Reederi	.. ..	Gm.(W)
221	Hilmar Reksten	.. ..	Nr.
†222	Silvertown Services Shipping, Ltd.	..	G.B.
223	Danske Kulkompagni A/S	..	Dk.
224	Franz L. Nimtz	..	Gm.(W)
225	Sandnaes D/S A/S ..	..	Nr.
226	Wolfgang Lattmann	..	Gm.(W)
227	Naviera del Nalon S.A.	..	Sp.
228	Nissan Kisen K.K.	.. ..	Jp.
229	Okada Shosen Kaisha	..	Jp.
230	Naviera Alvargonzalez S.A.	..	Sp.
231	Naviera Pinillos S.A.	..	Sp.
232	C. T. Bowring & Co. Ltd. ..	..	G.B.
233	Heinrich Schmidt Reederi	..	Gm.(W)
234	Scindia Steam Navigation Co. Ltd.	..	I.
235	Burnett Steamship Co. Ltd.	..	G.B.
236	Borregaard, A/S	.. ..	Nr.
237	Rasmus F. Olsen	.. ..	Nr.
238	Erling Mortensen A/S	.. ..	Nr.
239	Naviera Compostela S.A.	..	Sp.
240	Hans Kiaer & Co. A/S	..	Nr.
241	Cie. Nouvelle de Nav. Busck	..	Fr.
242	Erich Drescher	.. ..	Gm.(W)
†243	Aamodts Tankrederi A/S	..	Nr.
244	Egon Oldendorff	.. ..	Gm.(W)
245	Gebr. Broere N.V. ..	..	Nd.

211 to 245

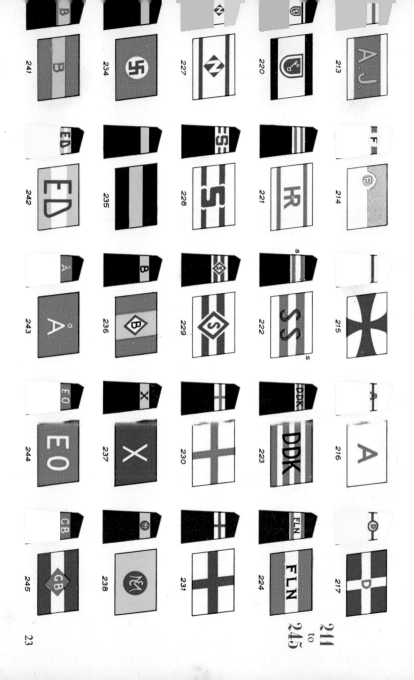

241. 234. 227. 220. 213.

242. 235. 228. 221. 214.

243. 236. 229. 222. 215.

244. 237. 230. 223. 216.

245. 238. 231. 224. 217.

211 to 245

No.	Company	Country
246	Polena, Soc. di Navigazione	Iy.
247	Ove Skou	Dk.
248	Onesimus Dorey & Sons Ltd.	G.B.
249	Grangesberg-Oxelosund Trafik A/B	Sw.
†250	Vesta Maritime Corpn. (Inglessis Subsidiary)	Lb.
251	Cia. Espanola de Petroleos S.A.	Sp.
252	Prebensen & Blakstad	Nr.
253	Einar Rasmussen	Nr.
254	Flensburger Trampreeder GmbH	Gm.(W)
255	Van Uden's Scheepvaart en Agentuur Maats.	Nd.
256	A. P. Moller (Maersk Line)	Dk.
257	Cia. Nav. Espanola S.A.	Sp.
258	D. J. Fafalios	Gc.
259	Sheaf S.S. Co. Ltd.	G.B.
260	Vesteraalens Dampskibsselskab A/S	Nr.
261	Matsuoka Kisen K.K.	Jp.
262	John Stewart & Co. Shipping Ltd.	G.B.
263	Armement Belgia S.A.	Bl.
264	C. Clausen	Dk.
265	Firth Shipping Co. Ltd.	G.B.
266	Finland-Sydamerika Linjen A/B	Fi.
267	Calmar S.S. Corpn.	U.S.A.
268	Hellenic Lines Ltd.	Gc.
269	Fenno S.S. Ltd., O/Y	Fi.
270	Gennaro Jacomino	Iy.
271	Rederi A/B Houtskar	Fi.
272	H. Peters	Gm.(W)
273	Iron Mines Co. of Venezuela	Ve.
274	John Nurminen O/Y	Fi.
275	Olympic Steamship Co. Inc.	U.S.A.
276	Penn Shipping Co. Inc.	U.S.A.
277	Union Navale	Fr.
278	West Coast Steamship Co.	U.S.A.
279	Axel Axelson Johnson	Sw.
280	Marina Mercante Nicaraguense S.A.	Ni.

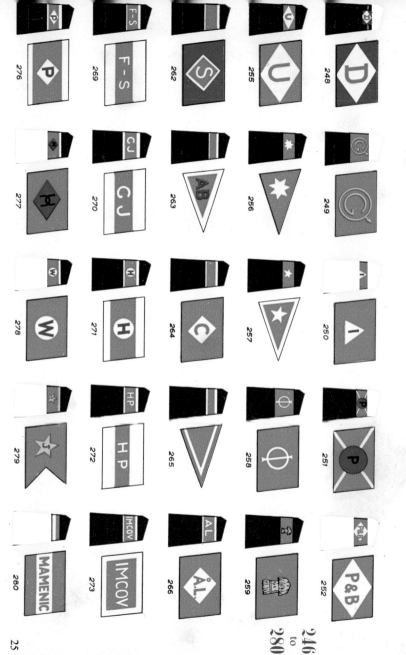

276 P

269 F-S

262 S

255 U

248 D

277 H

270 GJ

263 AB

256

249 Q

278 W

271 H

264 C

257

250 I

279

272 HP

265 V

258

251 P

280 MAMENIC

273 IMCOV

266 A.L.

259

252 P&B

246 to 280

25

281 to 315

No.	Company	Country
281	Dene Shipping Co. Ltd.	G.B.
282	Hakon A. Reuter	Sw.
283	Kvarnerska Plovidba	Yu.
284	Rob. M. Sloman Jr.	Gm.(W)
285	Bernhard Schulte	Gm.(W)
286	Texaco Inc.	U.S.A.
287	Arnold Thyselius	Gm.(W)
288	Pakistan Steam Navigation Co. Ltd.	P.
289	Chr. J. Reim	Nr.
290	Halcyon Lijn N.V.	Nd.
291	Porta Hamburger Reederei, GmbH	Gm.(W)
292	Fisser & v. Doornum	Gm.(W)
293	Mil Tankrederi A/S	Nr.
294	'Invotra' Invoer-en Transportonderneming	Nd.
295	Soc. d'Armement Fluvial et Maritime	Fr.
296	Vereenigde Nederlandsche Scheepvaart Maats.	Nd.
297	Nederlandse Erts-Tankers Maats, N.V.	Nd.
298	Itaya Shosen K.K.	Jp.
299	Hinode Kisen K.K.	Jp.
300	Forenede Dampskibs-Selskab A/S	Dk.
301	Nouvelle Cie. Havraise Peninsulaire de Nav.	Fr.
302	E. B. Aaby's Rederi A/S	Nr.
303	Asahi Kaiun K.K.	Jp.
304	Ivarans Rederi A/S Ivar. An. Christensen	Nr.
305	R. Fischer-Nielsen	Dk.
306	Gotland Angfartygsaktiebolaget	Sw.
307	Armement L. Hermans	Bl.
308	A. F. Klaveness & Co.	Nr.
309	Maritime Shipping & Trading Co. Ltd.	G.B.
310	Rud. Christ. Gribel	Gm.(W)
311	W. J. Tatem Ltd.	G.B.
312	Vrachtvaart N.V. Maats	Nd.
313	Lufti Yelkenci	Tk.
314	J. A. Zachariassen & Co.	Fi.
315	Iver Bugge	Nr.

26

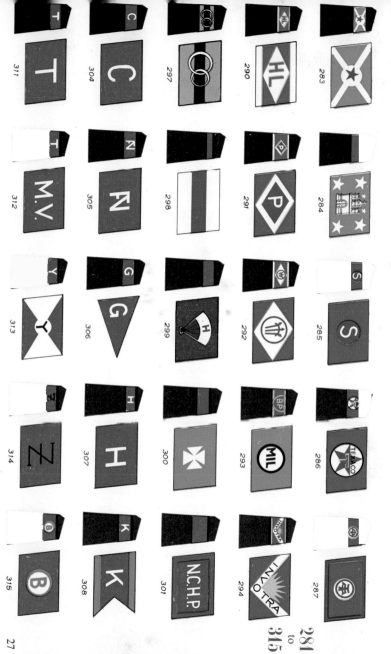

311   T

304   C

297

290   HL

283

312   M.V.

305   FN

298

291   P

284

313   Y

306   G

299   H

292

285   S

314   N

307   H

300

293   MIL

286   TEXACO

315   B

308   K

301   N.C.H.P.

294   INVO TRA

287

281 to 315

27

316	Warwick Tanker Co. Ltd.	.. ::	G.B.
317	Comben, Longstaff & Co. Ltd.	.. ::	G.B.
318	Hargreaves Coal & Shipping Ltd.	..	G.B.
319	Jorgen P. Jensen	.. ::	Nr.
320	Per Lodding ..	.. ::	Nr.
321	Mathies Reederei Kommanditgesellschaft		Gm.(W)
322	Naess Shipping Co. Inc.	.. ::	Various
323	Thesen's S.S. Co. Ltd.	.. ::	S.A.
324	Gustaf B. Thorden	.. ::	Sw.
325	India Steamship Co. Ltd.	.. ::	I.
326	Houlder Line Ltd.	.. ::	G.B.
327	Alexander Shipping Co. Ltd.	..	G.B.
328	Fearnley & Eger	.. ::	Nr.
329	Joseph Robinson & Sons (Management) Ltd.	..	G.B.
330	Dominion Shipping Co. Ltd.	..	C.
331	Severn Shipping Co. Ltd.	.. ::	G.B.
332	Union of Burma Shipping Board	..	Bm.
†333	Merchant Fleet of Union of Soviet Socialist Republics	..	U.S.S.R.
334	Tschudi & Eitzen	.. ::	Nr.
335	Altos Hornos de Vizcaya, S.A.	..	Sp.
336	Bornholm af 1886 A/S/D/S	..	Dk.
337	Anton von der Lippe	.. ::	Nr.
†338	Anders Jahre..	.. ::	Nr.
339	J. B. Stang	.. ::	Nr.
340	Constants Ltd.	.. ::	G.B.
341	Nordenfjeldske Dampskibsselskab A/S		Nr.
342	Mogul Line Ltd.	.. ::	I.
343	P. Brown Jun. & Co.	.. ::	Dk.
344	Hindustan S.S. Co. Ltd.	..	G.B.
345	Hinomaru Kisen K.K.	.. ::	Jp.
346	Heiwa Kisen K.K.	.. ::	Jp.
347	Karl Grammerstorf	.. ::	Gm.(W)
348	Luckenbach Steamship Co. Inc.	..	U.S.A.
349	Wm. H. Muller & Co. N.V.	..	Nd.
350	Peter Dohle	.. ::	Gm.(W)

316
to
350

28

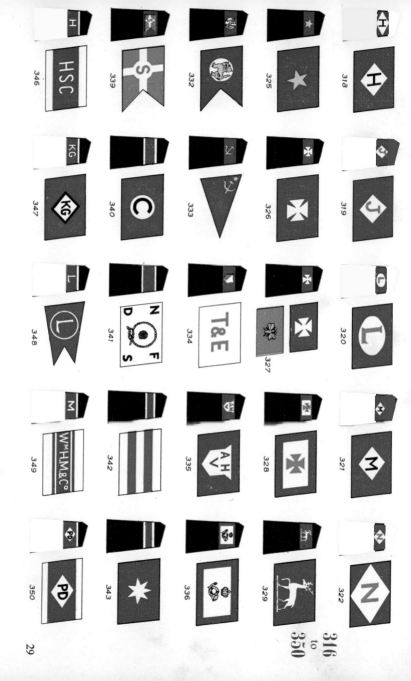

346 HSC
339 S
332
325 ★
318 H

347 KG
340 C
333
326 ✠
319 J

348 L
341 N D O F S
334 T&E
327 ✠
320 L

349 WᵐH.M.&Cº
342
335 A H V
328 ✠
321 M

350 PD
343 ✦
336
329
322 N

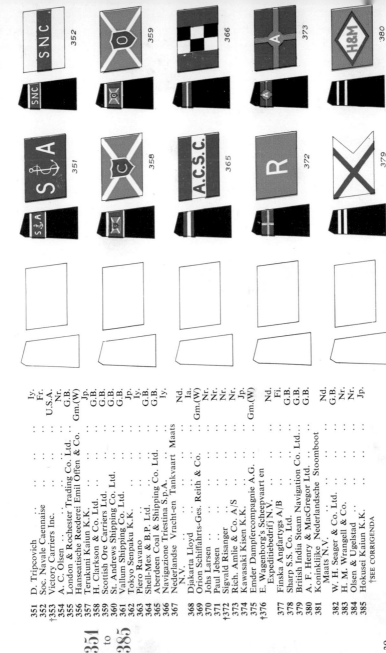

351	D. Tripcovich	Iy.
352	Soc. Navale Caennaise	Fr.
†353	Victory Carriers Inc.	U.S.A.
354	A. C. Olsen	Nr.
355	London & Rochester Trading Co. Ltd.	G.B.
356	Hanseatische Reederei Emil Offen & Co.	Gm.(W)
357	Terukuni Kaiun K.K.	Jp.
358	H. Clarkson & Co. Ltd.	G.B.
359	Scottish Ore Carriers Ltd.	G.B.
360	St. Andrews Shipping Co. Ltd.	G.B.
361	Vallum Shipping Co. Ltd.	G.B.
362	Tokyo Senpaku K.K.	Jp.
363	Piero Ravano	Iy.
364	Shell-Mex & B.P. Ltd.	G.B.
365	Aberdeen Coal & Shipping Co. Ltd.	G.B.
366	Navigazione Triestina S.p.A.	Iy.
367	Nederlandse Vracht-en Tankvaart Maats N.V.	Nd.
368	Djakarta Lloyd	Ia.
369	Orion Schiffahrts-Ges. Reith & Co.	Gm.(W)
370	Johs Larsen	Nr.
371	Paul Jebsen	Nr.
†372	Sigvald Risanger	Nr.
373	Rich. Amlie & Co. A/S	Nr.
374	Kawasaki Kisen K.K.	Jp.
375	Emder Dampfercompagnie A.G.	Gm.(W)
†376	E. Wagenborg's Scheepvaart en Expeditiebedrijf N.V.	Nd.
377	Finska Angfartygs A/B	Fi.
378	Sharp S.S. Co. Ltd.	G.B.
379	British India Steam Navigation Co. Ltd.	G.B.
380	A. F. Henry & MacGregor Ltd.	G.B.
381	Koninklijke Nederlandsche Stoomboot Maats N.V.	Nd.
382	W. H. Seager & Co. Ltd.	G.B.
383	H. M. Wrangell & Co.	Nr.
384	Olsen & Ugelstad	Nr.
385	Hokusei Kaiun K.K.	Jp.

†SEE CORRIGENDA

351 to 385

30

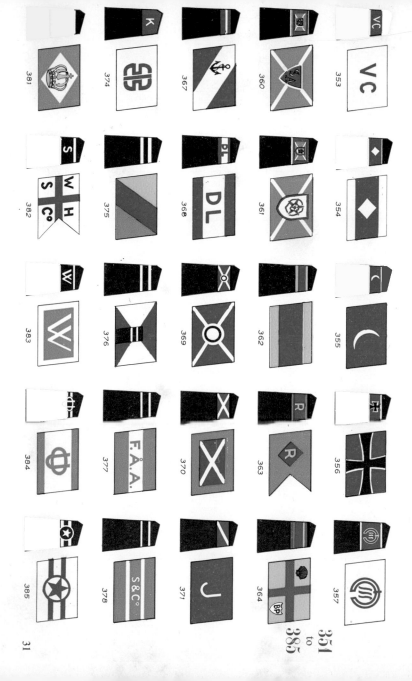

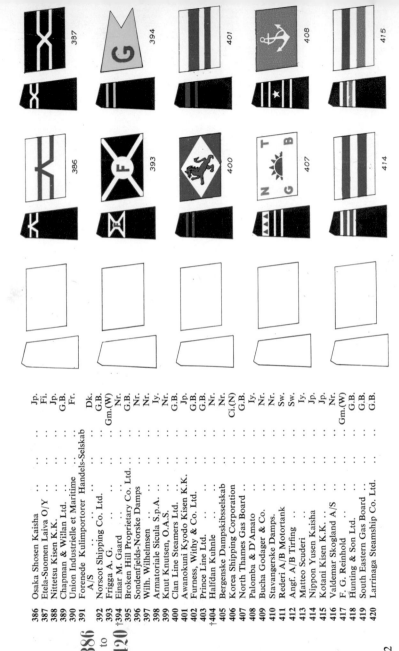

386	Osaka Shosen Kaisha	Jp.
387	Etela-Suomen Laiva O/Y	Fi.
388	Niitetsu Kisen K.K.	Jp.
389	Chapman & Willan Ltd.	G.B.
390	Union Industrielle et Maritime	Fr.
391	Forenede Kulimportorer Handels-Selskab A/S	Dk.
392	Norscot Shipping Co. Ltd.	G.B.
393	Frigga A. G.	Gm.(W)
†394	Einar M. Gaard	Nr.
395	Broken Hill Proprietary Co. Ltd.	G.B.
396	Sondenfjelds-Norske Damps	Nr.
397	Wilh. Wilhelmsen	Nr.
398	Armatoriale Sicula S.p.A.	Iy.
399	Knut Knutsen, O.A.S.	Nr.
400	Clan Line Steamers Ltd.	G.B.
401	Awanokuni Kyodo Kisen K.K.	Jp.
402	Furness, Withy & Co. Ltd.	G.B.
403	Prince Line Ltd.	G.B.
†404	Halfdan Kuhnle	Nr.
405	Bergenske Dampskibsselskab	Nr.
406	Korea Shipping Corporation	Ci.(N)
407	North Thames Gas Board	G.B.
408	Palomba & D'Amato	Iy.
409	Bucha Godager & Co.	Nr.
410	Stavangerske Damps.	Nr.
411	Rederi A/B Motortank	Sw.
412	Angf. A/B Tirfing	Sw.
413	Matteo Scuderi	Iy.
414	Nippon Yusen Kaisha	Jp.
415	Kotani Kisen K.K.	Jp.
416	Valdemar Skogland A/S	Nr.
417	F. G. Reinhold	Gm.(W)
418	Hunting & Son Ltd.	G.B.
419	South Eastern Gas Board	G.B.
420	Larrinaga Steamship Co. Ltd.	G.B.

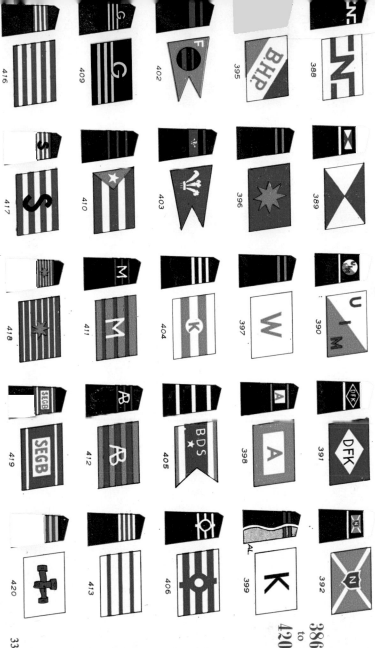

416

409 G
G

402 F

395 BHP

388 LN
LN

417 S
S

410

403

396

389

418

411 M
M

404 K

397 W

390 U
J
M

419 SEGB
SEGB

412 AB
AB

405 BDS

398 A
A

391 DFK
DFK

420

413

406

399 AL. K

392 N

421	T. & J. Brocklebank Ltd.	G.B.
422	Atlantic-Rhederei F. & W. Joch	Gm.(W)
423	British Oil Shipping Co. Ltd.	G.B.
424	Georg Vefling	Nr.
425	Neptun Dampfs. Gesellschaft	Gm.(W)
426	Bamburgh Shipping Co. Ltd.	G.B.
427	H. P. Vith	Gm.(W)
428	Daido Kaiun K.K.	Jp.
429	Poseidon Schiffahrt G.m.b.H.	Gm.(W)
430	Hugo Stinnes Transozean Schiffahrt	Gm.(W)
431	Tyne-Tees S.S. Co. Ltd.	G.B.
432	Kyle Shipping Co. Ltd.	G.B.
433	Panamanian Oriental S.S. Corpn.	Pa.
434	Koehn & Bohlmann Reederei K.G.	Gm.(W)
435	Petrofina S.A.	Bl.
436	Francisco Garcia, S.A.	Sp.
437	Limerick Steamship Co. Ltd.	Ei.
438	Schulte & Bruns	Gm.(W)
439	Hans Gjerpen & Co.	Nr.
440	Newry & Kilkeel S.S. Co. Ltd.	G.B.
441	John Kelly Ltd.	GB.
442	Regent Petroleum Tankship Co. Ltd.	G.B.
443	Cie de Navigation d'Orbigny	Fr.
444	Valck & Monckton, Cia. Maritima S.A.	Ch.
445	Suisse-Outremer S.A. de Gerance et d'Affretement Maritimes	Sz.
446	Strick Line Ltd.	G.B.
447	Karl Gross	Gm.(W)
448	Erich Retzlaff	Gm.(W)
449	Johann Haltermann	Gm.(W)
450	H. P. Vith & A. Hansen G.m.b.H.	Gm.(W)
451	Richard Schröder Reederei	Gm.(W)
452	Ernst Komrowski Reederei	Gm.(W)
453	Atlas Levante-Linie A.G.	Gm.(W)
454	Johannes Ick	Gm.(W)
455	Stener S. Muller	Nr.

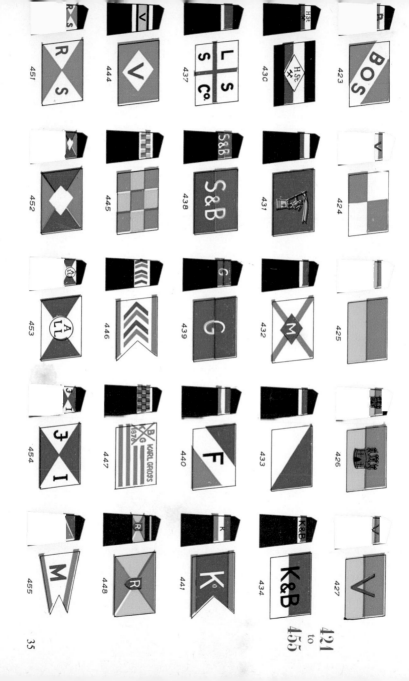

451 452 453 454 455

444 445 446 447 448

437 438 439 440 441

430 431 432 433 434

423 424 425 426 427

No.	Company		Country
456	Petroleos Mexicanos	:	Mx.
457	Witherington & Everett	:	G.B.
458	Cie Auxiliare de Navigation	:	Fr.
459	Bruusgaard Kiosterud & Co.	:	Nr.
460	Cie Nantaise des Chargeurs de l'Ouest	:	Fr.
461	Villain & Fassio e Cia Internazionale di Genova—Soc. Riunite di Nav.	:	Iy.
462	Corporacion Peruana de Vapores	:	Pu.
463	{Rederi A/B Bifrost	:	Sw.
	{Jarl R. Trapp	:	
464	Tamai Shosen K.K.	:	Jp.
465	Shimazu Kaiun K.K.	:	Jp.
466	Splosna Plovba	:	Yu.
467	Yacimientos Petroliferos Fiscales	:	Ar.
468	Rederiet Northsea I/S	:	Dk.
469	T.S. Bendixen	:	Nr.
470	Billners Rederi A/B	:	Sw.
471	Nerdrum Shipping Ltd.	:	G.B.
†472	Jacob Odland	:	Nr.
473	Sprague Steamship Co.	:	U.S.A.
474	Ditta G. M. Barbagelata	:	Iy.
475	De Vries & Co.	:	Gm.(W)
476	A/S Thor Dahl	:	Nr.
477	Administracion Nacional de Combustibles Alcohol y Portland	:	Uy.
478	Cia. Sicula di Armamento, S.p.A. Cosarma	:	Iy.
479	Shinnihon Kisen K.K.	:	Jp.
480	P. Meyer	:	Nr.
481	Mitsui Senpaku K.K.	:	Jp.
482	Ore Carriers of Liberia, Inc.	:	Lb.
483	Alcoa S.S. Co. Inc.	:	U.S.A.
484	Naviera Vizcaina S.A.	:	Sp.
485	South African Marine Corporation Ltd.	:	S.A.
486	Flota Mercante Grancolombiana S.A.	:	Co.
487	Ahlmann-Carlshutte K.G.	:	Gm.(W)
488	Flota Mercante Gran Centroamericana	:	Gu.
489	Van Geest, N.V. Waling, en Zonen	:	Nd.
490	Zim Israel Nav. Co. Ltd.	:	Is.

456 to 490

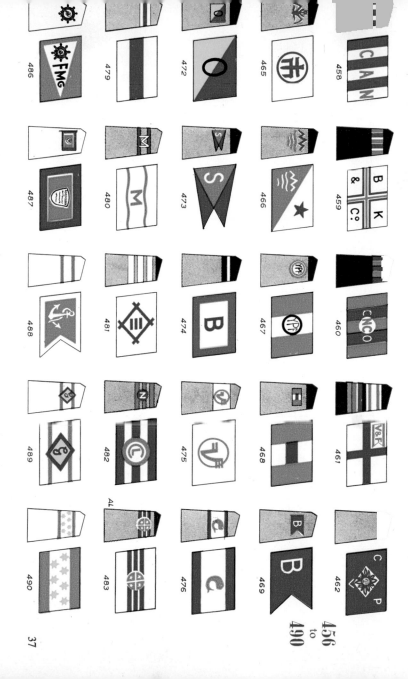

486

479

472

465

487

480

473

466

459

488

481

474

467

460

489

482

475

468

461

490

483

476

469

462

456 to 490

491   492   498   499   505   506   512   513   519   520

No.	Company	Country
491	Thai Maritime Navigation Co. Ltd.	Th.
492	Heinrich C. Horn	Gm.(W)
493	W. Holyman & Sons Propty Ltd.	A.
494	Anchor Shipping & Foundry Co. Ltd.	N.Z.
495	Cia de Navegacao Carregadores Acoreanos	Pg.
496	Northern Steam Ship Co. Ltd.	N.Z.
497	British & Continental Steamship Co. Ltd.	G.B.
498	Lloyd Brasileiro (Patrimonio Nacional)	Bz.
499	Australian Steamships Proprietary Ltd.	A.
500	Helmsing & Grimm.	Gm.(W)
501	Hamburg-Sudamerikanische Damps.	Gm.(W)
502	Sig Bergesen d.y. & Co.	Nr.
503	Leif Hoegh & Co.	Nr.
504	Austasia Line Ltd.	G.B.
505	Ragnar Brunkman	Sw.
506	A/S Det Dansk-Franske D/S	Dk.
507	Kavounides Shipping Co. Ltd.	Gc.
508	Burmah Oil Co. (Tankers) Ltd.	G.B.
509	Jadranska Linijska Plovidba	Yu.
510	Svenska Lloyd Rederi A/B.	Sw.
511	Gorthons Rederier	Sw.
512	Allan, Black & Co. Ltd.—Albyn Line Ltd.	G.B.
513	Soc. Siciliana Servizi Marittimi	Iy.
514	Brodarsko Poduzece Zadar	Yu.
515	Chimigas Marittima Cia. di Nav.	Iy.
516	Straits Steamship Co. Ltd.	G.B.
517	Petroleo Brasileiro—Petrobras	Bz.
518	Mariano Maresca & Co.	Iy.
519	Tirrenia, Soc. per Azioni di Navigazione	Iy.
520	Islands H/F Eimskipafelag	Ic.
521	B. Holter-Sorensen & Co.	Nr.
522	Carlo Cameli	Iy.
†523	Khedivial Mail Line, S.A.E.	Eg.
524	Graig Shipping Co. Ltd.	G.B.
525	Samband Islenzkra Samvinnufelaga	Ic.

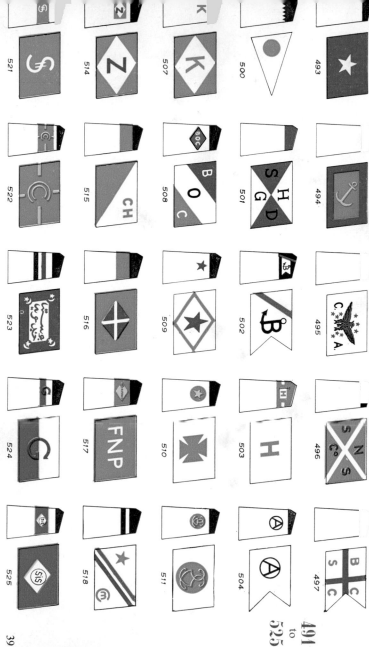

521
514
507
500
493

522
515
508
501
494

523
516
509
502
495

524
517
510
503
496

525
518
511
504
497

491
to
525

No.	Company	Country
526	Italia Soc. per Azioni di Navigazione	Iy.
527	Giuseppe Donato fu Lorenzo	Iy.
528	Rudolf A. Oetker	Gm.(W)
529	Cia. di Nav. Giuseppe Mazzini	Iy.
530	Fassio, Societa di Navigazione	Iy.
†531	Liverpool & North Wales Steamship Co. Ltd.	G.B.
532	Elder Dempster Lines Ltd.	G.B.
533	Royal Mail Lines Ltd.	G.B.
534	Orient Steam Navigation Col Ltd.	G.B.
535	Pacific Steam Navigation Co.	G.B.
536	Cie Maritime Belge (Lloyd Royal)	Bl.
537	North of Scotland, Orkney & Shetland Shipping Co. Ltd.	G.B.
538	Isthmian Lines Inc.	U.S.A.
539	MacAndrews & Co. Ltd.	G.B.
540	Asiastic Steam Navigation Co. Ltd.	G.B.
541	Australian-Oriental Line Ltd.	G.B.(H.K.)
542	Cable & Wireless Ltd.	G.B.
†543	New Zealand Shipping Co. Ltd.	G.B.
544	Canterbury Steam Shipping Co. Ltd.	N.Z.
545	Huddart Parker Ltd.	A.
†546	Navegacao Riograndense Ltda.	Bz.
547	Armenent Deppe, S.A.	Bl.
548	Commercial Cable Co. Ltd.	G.B.
549	F. Laeisz	Gm.(W)
550	Lyle Shipping Co. Ltd.	G.B.
551	All America Cables & Radio Inc.	U.S.A.
552	Ostasiatiske Kompagni A/S	Dk.
553	Norddeutscher Lloyd	Gm.(W)
554	Ben Line Steamers Ltd.	G.B.
555	Richard W. Jones & Co.	G.B.
556	Naviera Aznar S.A.	Sp.
557	Greek South American Line Shipping Co. S.A.	Gc.
558	Th. Joh. Kyvik	Nr.
559	Alva S.S. Co. Ltd.	G.B.
560	Oranje Lijn (Maatschappij Zeetransport) NV	Nd.

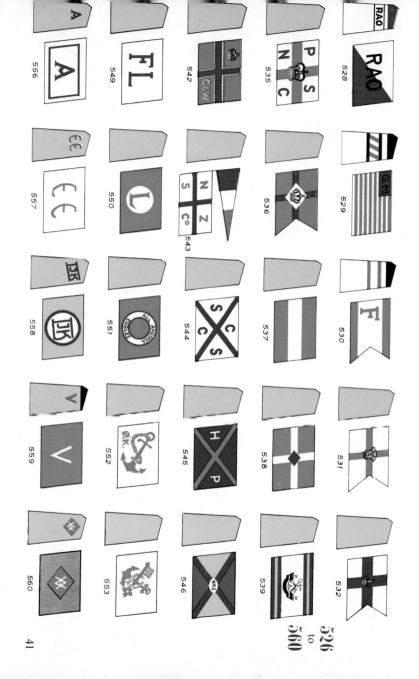

556 A

549 FL

542 C&W

535 P S N C

528 RAO

557 E E

550 L

543 S N Z Z S Co

536

529 GM

558 IJK

551 ALL AMERICA CABLES

544 C S C S

537

530 F

559 V

552 O.K.

545 H P

538

531

560

553

546 NRG

539 P

532

561	Coral Shipping Ltd.	..	..	Gc. Lb.
562	Cathay Shipping Co. Ltd.	..	..	G.B.
563	Ho Chiang Shipping Co. Ltd.	..	..	G.B.
564	Einar Saanum	..	..	Nr.
565	Flensburger Schiffsparten-Vereinigung A.G.	..	..	Gm.(W)
566	D'Amico Fratelli	..	..	Iy.
567	Argus S.S. Co. Inc.	..	..	Lb.
568	Svenska Rederi A/B Oresund	..	..	Sw.
569	Bowater S.S. Co. Ltd.	..	..	G.B.
570	Sten A. Olsson	..	..	Sw.
571	A/B Svenska Amerika Linien	..	..	Sw.
572	A/B Svenska Ostasiatiska Kompaniet	..	..	Sw.
573	M. Jebsen	..	..	Dk.
574	Christian F. Ahrenkiel	..	..	Gm.(W)
575	Euxine Shipping Co. Ltd.	..	..	G.B.
576	Louis Martin & Cie.	..	..	Fr.
577	Canadian Pacific Steamships Ltd.	..	..	G.B.
578	New Medway Steam Packet Co. Ltd.	..	..	G.B.
579	Thomas Watson (Shipping) Ltd.	..	..	G.B.
580	L. Harboe Jensen & Co.	..	..	Nr.
581	J. F. Farsjo & Co.	..	..	Nr.
582	Olsen Brodrene A/S	..	..	Nr.
583	Leif Erichsen	..	..	Nr.
584	Fred Olsen & Co.	..	..	Nr.
585	Jacob Lind	..	..	Nr.
586	Eilert Lund	..	..	Nr.
587	Alf Mohn Jr.	..	..	Nr.
588	Harry Borthen & Co. A/S	..	..	Nr.
589	Alexander Bech	..	..	Nr.
590	Ludv. G. Braathen	..	..	Nr.
591	Th. Brovig	..	..	Nr.
592	Anders Borresen	..	..	Nr.
596	Les Cargos Algeriens	..	..	Fr.
594	Herm. Dauelsberg	..	..	Gm.(W)
595	Cie. Belge d'Expansion Maritime, S.A.	..	..	Bl.

561 to 595

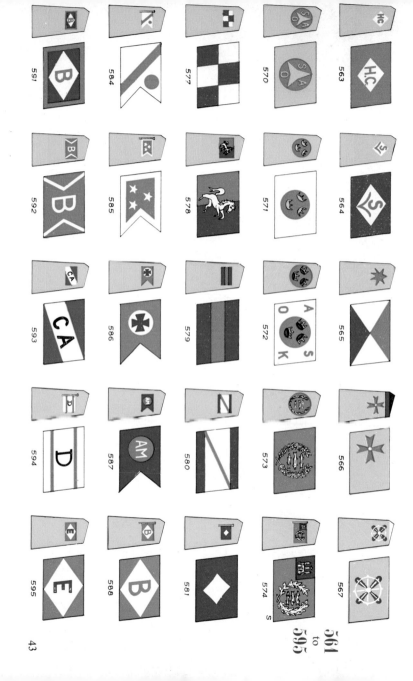

591
584
577
570
563

592
585
578
571
564

593
586
579
572
565

594
587
580
573
566

595
588
581
574
567

561
to
595

597

604

611

618

625

596

603

610

617

624

596	Erik Seyd Frachtschiffahrt	..	Gm.(W)
597	Johan Gerrard	..	Nr.
598	C. T. Gogstad & Co.	..	Nr.
599	Gerner Mathisen Rederi A/S	..	Nr.
†600	Christian Haaland	..	Nr.
601	Dagfin Henriksen	..	G.B.
602	Hull Gates Shipping Co. Ltd.	..	Nr.
603	Harald Stange & Co. A/S	..	Nr.
604	Ludvig Lorentzen	..	Gm.(W)
†605	Leo Adams Reederei	..	Pp.
606	Philippine St. Nav. Co.	..	Nr.
607	Bendt Rasmussen	..	Nr.
608	Olav Ringdal	..	Nr.
609	Robert Bartholomay	..	Gm.(W)
610	Marcus Chr. Stray	..	Nr.
611	S. Schanche	..	Nr.
612	Soc. Anonyme de Gerance et d'Armement	..	Fr.
613	Bristol St. Navigation Co. Ltd.	..	G.B.
614	Cie. Maritime de Transports de Goudron	..	Fr.
615	Haldor Virik	..	Nr.
616	Koninklijke Hollandsche Lloyd	..	Nd.
617	Brodrene Utkilens Rederi	..	Nr.
618	Peder Smedvig	..	Nr.
619	Cie. Maritime des Chargeurs Reunis, S.A.	..	Fr.
620	Norships Ocean Carriers Ltd.	..	G.B.
621	Antonios G. Pappadakis	..	Gc.
622	Bj. Ruud-Pedersen	..	Nr.
623	Jonny Wesch	..	Gm.(W)
624	Nederlandsch-Amerikaansche Stoomvaart Maatschappij N.V.	..	Nd.
625	Cia. Colonial de Navegacao	..	Pg.
626	Cie. de Transports Oceaniques	..	Fr.
627	Helmer Staubo & Co.	..	Nr.
628	Olistim Nav. Co. Ltd.	..	Le
629	Jorgen Bang	..	Nr,
630	Skanska Cement A/B	..	Sw.

596 to **630**

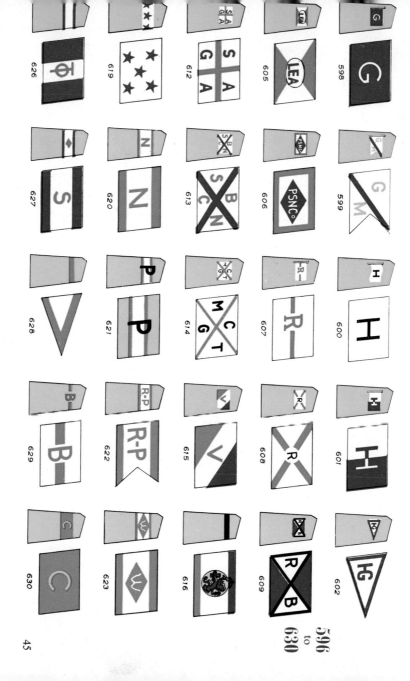

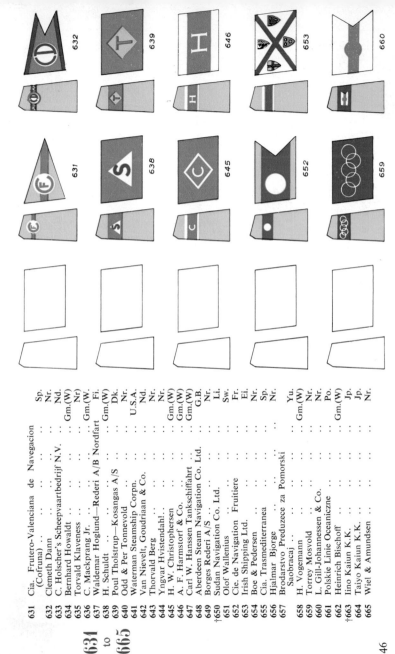

631	Cia. Frutero-Valenciana de Navegacion (Cofruna)	Sp.
632	Clemeth Dann	Nr.
633	C. Holscher's Scheepvaartbedrijf N.V. ..	Nd.
634	Bernhard Howaldt	Gm.(W)
635	Torvald Klaveness	Nr)
636	C. Mackprang Jr.	Gm.(W.
637	Waldemar Hoglund—Rederi A/B Nordfart	Fi.
638	H. Schuldt	Gm.(W)
639	Poul Tholstrup—Kosangas A/S	Dk.
640	Odd & Per Tonnevold	Nr.
641	Waterman Steamship Corpn.	U.S.A.
642	Van Nievelt, Goudriaan & Co.	Nd.
643	Thorvald Berg	Nr.
644	Yngvar Hvistendahl..	Nr.
645	H. W. Christophersen	Gm.(W)
646	A. F. Harmstorf & Co.	Gm.(W)
647	Carl W. Hanssen Tankschiffahrt	Gm.(W)
648	Aberdeen Steam Navigation Co. Ltd. ..	G.B.
649	Borges Rederi A/S	Nr.
†650	Sudan Navigation Co. Ltd.	Li.
651	Olof Wallenius	Sw.
652	Cie. de Navigation Fruitiere	Fr.
653	Irish Shipping Ltd.	Ei.
654	Boe & Pedersen	Nr.
655	Cia. Trasmediterranea	Sp.
656	Hjalmar Bjorge	Nr.
657	Brodarstvo Preduzece za Pomorski Saobracaj	Yu.
658	H. Vogemann	Gm.(W)
659	Torrey Mosvold	Nr.
660	L. Gill-Johannessen & Co.	Nr.
661	Polskie Linie Oceaniczne	Po.
662	Heinrich Bischoff	Gm.(W)
†663	Iino Kaiun K.K.	Jp.
664	Taiyo Kaiun K.K.	Jp.
665	Wiel & Amundsen	Nr.

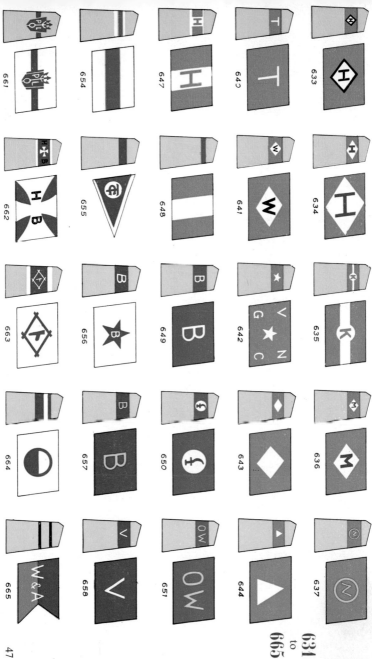

661   654   647   645   633

662   655   648   641   634

663   656   649   642   635

664   657   650   643   636

665   658   651   644   637

666	Rolf Wigands Rederi	Nr.
667	Reidar Rod	Nr.
668	Anders Willhemsen	Nr.
669	Erik O. Brodin	Sw.
670	Lundqvist Rederierna	Fi.
671	Cia. Anon. Venezolana de Navegacion	Ve.
672	Clarke Steamship Co. Ltd.	C.
673	Counties Ship Management Co. Ltd. and London & Overseas Freighters Ltd.	G.B.
674	Moltzau & Christensen	Nr.
675	Oldenburg-Portugiesische Dampschiffs-Rhederei	Gm.(W)
676	Navigazione Libera Giuliana S.p.A.	Iy.
677	Meridian Schiffahrtsges. m.b.H.	Gm.(W)
678	Skipautgerd Rikisins	Ic.
679	Jugoslavenska Tankerska Plovidba	Yu
680	Muhammadi Steamship Co. Ltd.	P.
681	Norske Amerikalinje A/S	Nr.
682	Wallem & Co. A/S	Nr.
683	C. H. Sorensen & Sonner	Nr.
684	Wallem Steckmest & Co. A/S	Nr.
685	Adelaide Steamship Co. Ltd.	A.
686	Haldin & Co. Ltd.—Court Line Ltd.	G.B.
687	King Line Ltd.	G.B.
688	Bank Line Ltd.	G.B.
689	Koninklijke Paketvaart Maats. N.V.	Nd.
690	Soc. Navale de l'Ouest	Fr.
691	Petromar S.R.L.	Iy.
692	Jacob Christensen	Nr.
693	Shaw Savill & Albion Co. Ltd.	G.B.
694	Surrey Shipping Co. Ltd.	G.B.
695	Booker Line Ltd.	G.B.
696	Smith's Coasters (Proprietary) Ltd.	S.A.
697	Empresa Insulana de Nav.	Pg.
698	Elders & Fyffes Ltd.	G.B.
699	Great Yarmouth Shipping Co. Ltd.	G.B.
700	H. Hogarth & Sons Ltd.	G.B.

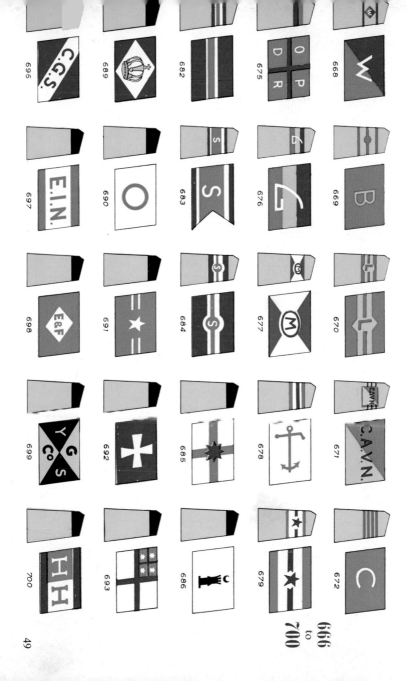

695

689

682

675

668 W

697 E.I.N.

690 O

683 S

676

669 B

698 E&F

691

684 S

677 M

670 L

699 Y G Co S

692

685

678

671 C.A.V.N.

700 HH

693

686 C

679

672 C

666 to 700

49

701	Hollandsche Stoomboot Maats. N.V.	Nd.
702	Hudig & Pieters' Algemeene Scheep. Maats. N.V.	Nd.
703	H. M. Gehrckens	Gm.(W)
704	John I. Jacobs & Co. Ltd.	G.B.
705	Nederland N.V. Stoomvaart Maatschappij	Nd.
706	Cie. de Nav. Sud Atlantique	Fr.
707	Richardson & Co. Ltd.	N.Z.
708	Sartori & Berger	Gm.(W)
709	United Africa Co. Ltd.	G.B.
710	Zillah Shipping Co. Ltd.	G.B.
711	British Railways Board (late B.T.C.)	G.B.
712	Transatlantic Rederiaktiebolaget	Sw.
713	British Phosphate Commissioners	G.B.
714	Biorn Biornstad & Co.	Nr.
715	T.N. Epiphaniades Shipping Co. Ltd.	Gc.
716	Costa, Giacomo fu Andrea	Iy.
717	Erik Bancks Rederi A/B	Sw.
718	West Hartlepool St. Navigation Co. Ltd.	G.B.
719	Thorvald Hansen	Nr.
720	August Kjerland & Co.	Nr.
721	Lauritz Kloster	Nr.
722	Matson Navigation Co.	U.S.A.
723	Oceanic Steamship Co.	U.S.A.
724	O. Gross & Sons Ltd.	G.B.
725	C. Rowbotham & Sons (Management) Ltd.	G.B.
726	Stephens, Sutton Ltd.	G.B.
727	Typaldos Brothers Steamship Co. Ltd.	Gc.
728	Christian F. Bonnevie	Nr.
729	N. Chr. Evensen	Nr.
730	Hopemount Shipping Co. Ltd.—Stott, Mann & Co.	G.B.
731	Harries Bros. & Co. Ltd.	G.B.
732	Hemsley Bell Ltd.	G.B.
733	Hans Kruger	Gm.(W)
734	Hadley Shipping Co. Ltd.	G.B.
735	Andrea Marsano & Sons	Iy.

731 HB&C° LTD

724 O↓G

717 EB

710 Z

703 H.M.G.

732 H B

725 R

718 ✝

711

704 ✡

733 HK

726 R

719 ⅢⅢ

712 A R T B

705 N

734 HSC

727

720 K

713 B.P.C.

706 ◇

735 M

728 Ⓑ

721 K

714 B

707 R & C°

701 to 735

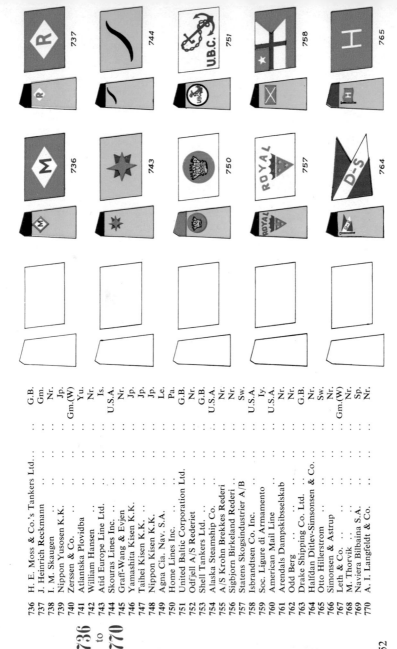

736	H. E. Moss & Co.'s Tankers Ltd.	..	:	G.B.
737	J. Heinrich Reckmann	..	:	Gm.
738	I. M. Skaugen	..	:	Nr.
739	Nippon Yusosen K.K.	..	:	Jp.
740	Zerssen & Co.	..	:	Gm.(W)
741	Atlantska Plovidba		:	Yu.
742	William Hansen	..	:	Nr.
743	Atid Europe Line Ltd.		:	Is.
744	Skouras Lines Inc.	..	:	U.S.A.
745	Graff-Wang & Evjen		:	Nr.
746	Yamashita Kisen K.K.		:	Jp.
747	Taihei Kisen K.K.	..	:	Jp.
748	Nippon Kisen K.K.		:	Jp.
749	Agna Cia. Nav. S.A.		:	Le.
750	Home Lines Inc.	..	:	Pa.
751	United Baltic Corporation Ltd.		:	G.B.
752	Odfjell A/S Rederiet		:	Nr.
753	Shell Tankers Ltd.	..	:	G.B.
754	Alaska Steamship Co.		:	U.S.A.
755	A/S Krohn Brekkes Rederi		:	Nr.
756	Sigbjørn Birkeland Rederi	..	:	Nr.
757	Statens Skogsindustrier A/B		:	Sw.
758	Isbrandtsen Co. Inc.	..	:	U.S.A.
759	Soc. Ligure di Armamento	..	:	Iy.
760	American Mail Line	..	:	U.S.A.
761	Arendals Dampskibsselskab		:	Nr.
762	Odd Berg	..	..	:	Nr.
763	Drake Shipping Co. Ltd.	..	:	G.B.
764	Halfdan Ditlev-Simsonsen & Co.	..	:	Nr.
765	Otto Hillerstrøm	..	:	Sw.
766	Simonsen & Astrup	..	:	Nr.
767	Leth & Co.	..	..	:	Gm.(W)
768	M. Thorvik	..	..	:	Nr.
769	Naviera Bilbaina S.A.	..	:	Sp.
770	A. I. Langfeldt & Co.	..	:	Nr.

736 to 770

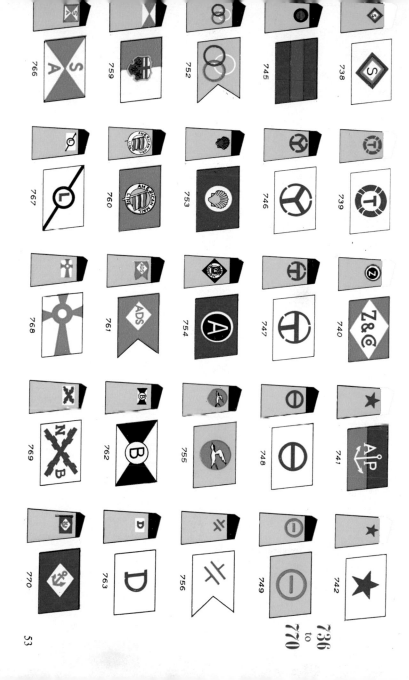

766   759   752   745   738

767   760   753   746   739

768   761   754   747   740

769   762   755   748   741

770   763   756   749   742

736 to 770

771	Farrell Lines Inc.	U.S.A.
772	City Line Ltd. (Ellerman's)	G.B.
773	Ellerman & Bucknall S.S. Co. Ltd.	G.B.
774	Hall Line Ltd. (Ellerman's)	G.B.
775	Ellerman & Papayanni Lines Ltd.	G.B.
776	Westcott & Laurence Line Ltd. (Ellerman's)	G.B.
777	James Fisher & Sons Ltd.	G.B.
778	United Vintners Inc.	U.S.A.
779	Okeanoporos Shipping Co. Ltd.	Gc.
780	Showa Yusosen K.K.	Jp.
781	Winchester Shipping Co. Ltd.	G.B.
782	British Channel Islands Shipping Co. Ltd.	G.B.
783	Ingvar Jansen	Nr.
784	A/S Arne Sveen's Rederi	Nr.
785	Helmut Bastian	Gm.(W)
786	Australind Steam Shipping Co. Ltd.	G.B.
787	Charrington Gardner Locket (London) Ltd.	G.B.
788	Ameritalia Soc. di Nav.	Iy.
789	Finn Wahlstrom	Nr.
790	Antti Wihuri	Fi.
791	Charlton S.S. Co. Ltd.	G.B.
792	American Union Transport Inc.	U.S.A.
793	Moore-McCormack Lines Inc.	U.S.A.
794	Argo Reederei Richard Adler & Sohne	Gm.(W)
795	Cie. Nouvelle France-Navigation	Fr.
796	Queenship Navigation Ltd.	G.B.
797	Associated Humber Lines Ltd.	G.B.
798	Hugh Craig & Co. Ltd.	G.B.
799	United Fruit Co.	U.S.A.
800	Melsom & Melsom	Nr.
801	Johan M. Ugland	Nr.
802	James Nourse Ltd.	G.B.
803	Hamburg-Amerika Linie	Gm.(W)
804	Adriatica Soc. per Azion di Nav.	Iy.
805	Coast Steamships Ltd.	A.

771 to 805

54

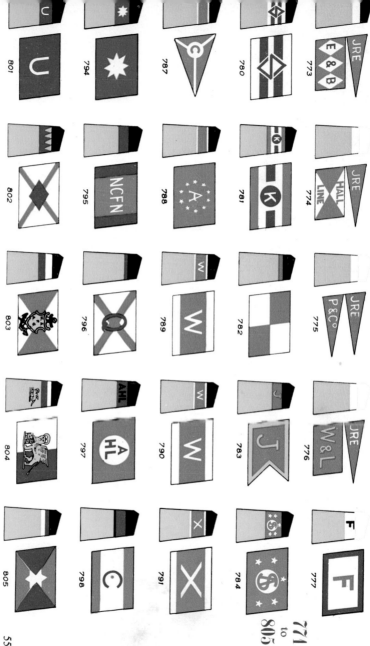

801
794
787
780
773 E & B / JRE

802
795 NCFN
788 A
781 K
774 HALL LINE / JRE

803
796
789 W
782
775 P & Cº / JRE

804
797 AHL
790 W
783 J
776 W & L / JRE

805
798
791 X
784
777 F

771 to 805

806	R. Nordstrom & Co.	Fi.
807	China Union Lines Ltd.	Ci.(N)
808	Delta Steamship Lines Inc.	U.S.A.
809	J. Ludwig Mowinckels Rederi A/S	Nr.
810	Tito Campanella Soc. Nav.	Iy.
811	Trinidad Corporation	U.S.A.
812	Marco U. Martinolich	Iy.
813	Rederi A/B Timex	Sw.
814	Roberto Andalo	Iy.
815	Belgian Fruit Lines, S.A.	Bl.
816	Lobitos Oilfields Ltd.	G.B.
817	Denizcilik Bankasi T.A.O.	Tk.
818	Arne Blystad	Nr.
819	Gennaro Montella	Iy.
820	Kornelius Olsen	Nr.
821	Montemar Soc. Anon. Comercial y Maritima	Uy.
822	Toho Kaiun K.K.	Jp.
823	Lloyd Triestino Soc. per Azioni di Nav.	Iy.
824	A. O. Andersen & Co's Eftf.	Nr.
825	A. E. Sorensen	Dk.
826	Angf. A/B Bore	Fi.
827	Onstad Shipping Co.	Nr.
828	Sigurd Herlofson & Co.	Nr.
829	Kjell Rinde	Nr.
830	Evan Thomas Radcliffe & Co. Ltd.	G.B.
831	C. K. Hansen	Dk.
832	S. H. Smith Sorensen	Nr.
833	N. V. Houtvaart	Nd.
834	Bachke & Co.	Nr.
835	Egil Naesheim	Nr.
836	Birger Pedersen & Sons Rederi A/S	Nr.
837	Eiv. Evensen	Nr.
838	Basse & Co.	Dk.
839	John P. Pedersen & Son	Nr.
840	Riboli & Spadiglieri	Iy.

836 P

829 R

822 H

815 B.F.L.

808

837 E

830

823

816 L O L

809 M

838 H

831

824

817

810

839 JPP&S

832

825 AES

818 B

811

840 R|S

833 H

826 B

819 M

812

806
to
840

841 to 875

841	Central Gulf Steamship Corpn.		U.S.A.
842	Deutsch Seereederei (V.E.B.)		Gm.(E)
843	Paulins Rederier		Fi.
844	Prudential Steamship Corpn.		U.S.A.
845	Westfal-Larsen & Co. A/S		Nr.
846	Sigurd Sorvig		Nr.
847	Italnavi Soc. di Navigazione per Azioni		Iy.
848	Keystone Shipping Co.		U.S.A.
849	Rederi A/B Clipper (Einar Hansen)		Sw.
850	Navigazione Mercantile S.p.A.		Iy.
851	Rederi A/B Malmoil		Sw.
852	Johan Rasmussen & Co.		Nr.
853	Berge Sigval Bergesen		Nr.
854	Brussels Steamship Co. Ltd.		G.B.
855	Magnus Konow & Co.		Nr.
856	Stoomv. Maats. Oostzee N.V.		Nd.
857	Maldivian Nationals Trading Corporation (Ceylon) Ltd.		Md.I.
858	Stoomb. Maats. Hillegersberg N.V.		Nd.
859	Nederlandse Maats. voor de Walvisvaart N.V.		Nd.
860	Black Star Line Ltd.		Gh.
861	A. K. Fernströms Rederi		Sw.
862	Weyerhaeuser S.S.Co.		U.S.A.
863	Belships Co. Ltd. (Christen Smith)		Nr.
864	Gulf Oil Corporation		U.S.A.
865	Grimaldi Fratelli		Iy.
866	A/S Borgestad		Nr.
867	Sveriges Oljekonsumenters Riksforbund		Sw.
868	Inui Kisen K.K.		Jp.
869	States Steamship Co.		U.S.A.
870	Pure Oil Co.		U.S.A.
871	Hudson Steamship Co. Ltd.		G.B.
872	Marine Transport Lines Inc.		U.S.A.
873	American President Lines Ltd.		U.S.A.
874	Naviera Chilena del Pacifico S.A.		Ch.
875	General Shipping Co. Inc.		Pp.

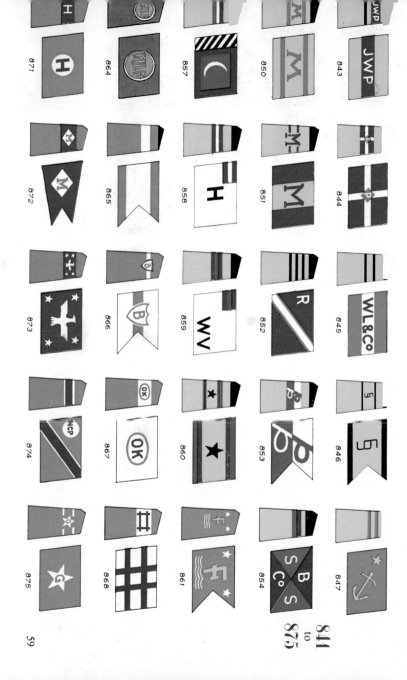

841
to
875

876	Peter Heering	..	..	..	Dk.
877	Pacific Far East Line Inc.	..	..	U.S.A.
878	Oceana Shipping, S.A.	..	..	Sz.
879	N. G. Livanos	..	..	..	Gc.
880	Gestioni Esercizio Navi Sicilia	..	Iy.
881	P. Bork Shipping A/S	..	..	Dk.
882	Alfred Holt & Co.—Blue Funnel Line	..	G.B.
883	Ocean Nederlandsche Stoomvaart Maats		
	N.V.	..	..	..	Nd.
884	Navigazione Alta Italia S.p.A.	..	Iy.
885	Raffaele Capano	..	..	Iy.
886	R.S. Dalgliesh Ltd.	..	..	G.B.
887	Sven Salen A/B	..	..	Sw.
888	Sicula Oceanica S.A.	..	..	Iy.
889	Stevinson Hardy (Tankers) Ltd.	..	G.B.
890	Ilva Alti Forni e Acciaierie d'Italia	..	Iy.
891	T. C. Christensen & Co.	..	..	Dk.
892	Achille Lauro	..	..	Iy.
893	Fanges & Pahlssons Rederier	..	Sw.
894	Soc. Navale Delmas-Vieljeux	..	Fr.
895	Imperial Chemical Industries Ltd.	..	G.B.
896	Jugoslavensko Recno Brodarstvo	..	Yu.
†897	Chowgule Steamships (Bahamas) Ltd.	G.B.
898	Atlantic Steam Navigation Co. Ltd.	G.B.
899	Lamport & Holt Line Ltd.	..	..	G.B.
900	Ditta Andrea Zanchi	..	..	Iy.
901	Australian Coastal Shipping Commission	A.
902	Jamaica Banana Producers S.S. Co. Ltd.	Jam. G.B.
903	American Oil Co.	..	..	U.S.A.
904	Rederi A/B Fraternitas	..	..	Sw.
905	Jugoslavenska Linijska Plovidba	..	Yu.
906	Mario Attanasio	..	..	Iy.
907	Bjorn G. Braathen	..	..	Nr.
908	Metcalf Motor Coasters Ltd.	..	G.B.
909	Otto Danielsen Rederiet	..	..	Dk.
910	Texas City Refining Inc.	..	..	U.S.A.

876 to 910

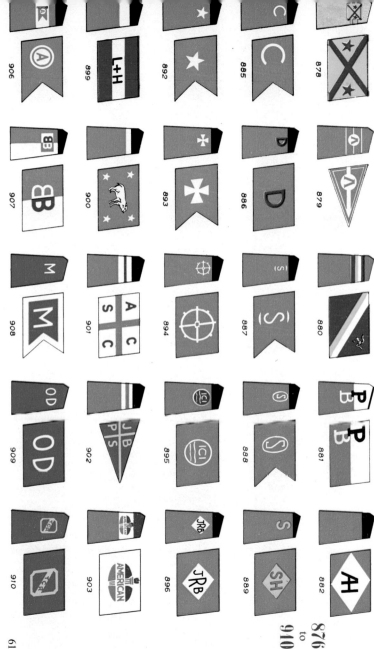

906
899
892
885
878

907
900
893
886
879

908
901
894
887
880

909
902
895
888
881

910
903
896
889
882

**876
to
910**

911	Hess Tankship Co.	U.S.A.
912	Sir R. Ropner & Co. Ltd.	G.B.
913	Kansai Kisen K.K.	Jp.
914	Federal Commerce & Navigation Co. Ltd.	C.
915	John Burke Ltd.	A.
916	Holm & Co. Ltd.	N.Z.
†917	Sugar Line Ltd.	G.B.
918	Oregon Steamship Co. Ltd.	G.B.
919	Grace Line Inc.	U.S.A.
†920	Transatlantic Carriers Ltd.	G.B.
921	Soc. Ivoirienne de Nav.	Iv. Coast
922	Gulf & South American Steamship Co. Inc.	U.S.A.
923	National Iranian Tanker Co. (Nederland) N.V.	Nd.
924	B.P. Clyde Tanker Co. Ltd.	G.B.
925	Nigerian National Line Ltd.	Ng.
926	Soc. Portuguesa de Navios Tanques Ltda (Soponata)	Pg.
927	Palm Line Ltd.	G.B.
928	Cia. Armatoriale Italiana	Iy.
929	J. Lauritzen	Dk.
930	Bloomfield Steamship Co.	U.S.A.
931	Andreas J. Zachariassen	Gm.(W)
932	McIlwraith McEacharn Ltd.	A.
933	Kyoei Tanker K.K.	Jp.
934	Central Electricity Generating Board	G.B.
935	Indo-China St. Navigation Co. Ltd.	G.B.
936	Southampton, Isle of Wight & South of England Royal Mail Steam Packet Co. Ltd. (Red Funnel Steamers Ltd.)	
937	David Macbrayne Ltd.	G.B.
938	Union-Castle Mail S.S. Co. Ltd.	G.B.
939	Glen Line Ltd.	G.B.
940	Belfast S.S. Co. Ltd.	G.B.
941	Febo Amedeo Bertorello	Iy.
942	Madrigal Shipping Co. Inc.	Pp.
943	A. Alfino & Figli	Iy.
944	African Coasters (Pty.) Ltd.	S.A.
945	Cia Sud-Americana de Vapores	Ch.

941 · 934 · 927 · 920 · 913
942 · 935 · 928 · 921 · 914
943 · 936 · 929 · 922 · 915
944 · 937 · 930 · 923 · 916
945 · 938 · 931 · 924 · 917

911 to 945

63

No.	Company	Country
946	Cie Generale Transatlantique	Fr.
947	Dundee, Perth & London Shipping Co. Ltd.	G.B.
948	Arthur Guinness, Son & Co. (Dublin) Ltd.	Ei.
†949	Glen & Co. Ltd.	G.B.
950	Guinea Gulf Line Ltd.	G.B.
951	Harrisons (Clyde) Ltd.	G.B.
952	Ellerman's Wilson Line Ltd.	G.B.
953	Angelo Scincariello	Iy.
954	Teck Hwa Shipping Co. Ltd.	G.B.
955	Osborn & Wallis Ltd.	G.B.
956	Bibby Line Ltd.	G.B.
957	Isle of Man Steam Packet Co. Ltd.	G.B.
958	Union Steam Ship Co. of New Zealand Ltd.	N.Z.
959	Port Line Ltd.	G.B.
960	P. MacCallum & Sons Ltd.	G.B.
961	Bland Line Ltd.	G.B.
†962	Cunard Steam-Ship Co. Ltd.	G.B.
963	Falkland Islands Trading Co. Ltd.	G.B.
964	Insa Societa di Navigazione (Giovanni Gavarone)	Iy.
965	West Wales S.S. Co. Ltd. (Gibbs & Co)	G.B.
966	Hugh Roberts & Son	G.B.
967	Sir William Reardon Smith & Sons Ltd.	G.B.
968	Svend Hellesen	Dk.
969	Halal Shipping Co. Ltd.	G.B.
970	Athel Line Ltd.	G.B.
971	Empressa Nacional Elcano de la Marina Mercante.	Sp.
972	Sabine Transportation Co. Inc.	U.S.A.
973	Garibaldi, Soc. Co-Operativa di Navigazione	Iy.
974	Hamburg-Atlantik Linie, GmbH	Gc.
975	Naviera Morey S.A.	Sp.
976	South American Saint Line Ltd.	G.B.
977	Federal Steam Navigation Co. Ltd.	G.B.
978	J. & J. Denholm Ltd.	G.B.
979	Mountwood Shipping Co. Ltd.	G.B.
980	Avenue Shipping Co. Ltd.	G.B.

981	Southern Line Ltd.	G.B.
982	Blue Star Line Ltd.	G.B.
983	Colombine Shipping Co.	Li.
984	Canada Steamship Lines Ltd.	C.
985	Joaquin Davila y Cia	Sp.
986	Trans Oceanic Steamship Co. Ltd.	P.
987	Hedwigshutte Kohlen und Kokswerke A.G.	Gc.
988	Red Rose Navigation Co. Ltd.	G.B.
989	Chr. Salvesen & Co. Ltd.	G.B.
990	United States Lines Co.	U.S.A.
991	Associated Anglo-Scandinavian Shipping Co. Ltd.	G.B.
992	Sinclair Refining Co.	U.S.A.
993	D. L. Street Ltd.	G.B.
994	Chine Shipping Co. Ltd. (Anglo-Danubian Transport Co. Ltd.)	G.B.
995	Geo. Nisbet & Co. Ltd.	G.B.
996	Burns & Laird Lines Ltd.	G.B.
997	J. R. Rix & Sons Ltd.	G.B.
998	Shamrock Shipping Co. Ltd.	G.B.
999	Soc. Anon. Importadora y Exportadora de la Patagonia	Ar.
1000	Soc. Belge de Navigation Maritime Navibel	Bl.
1001	B.P. Tanker Co. Ltd.	G.B.
1002	Cia. Chilena de Navegacion Interoceanica	Ch.
1003	Saint Line Ltd. (Mitchell Cotts & Co. Ltd.)	G.B.
1004	Hall Bros. S.S. Co. Ltd.	G.B.
1005	Manchester Liners Ltd.	G.B.
1006	Constantine Shipping Co. Ltd.	G.B.
1007	Cosulich, Fratelli	Iy.
1008	Trader Navigation Co. Ltd.	G.B.
1009	Charles Schiaffino et Cie	Fr.
1010	Cie. Asiatique de Navigation	Fr.

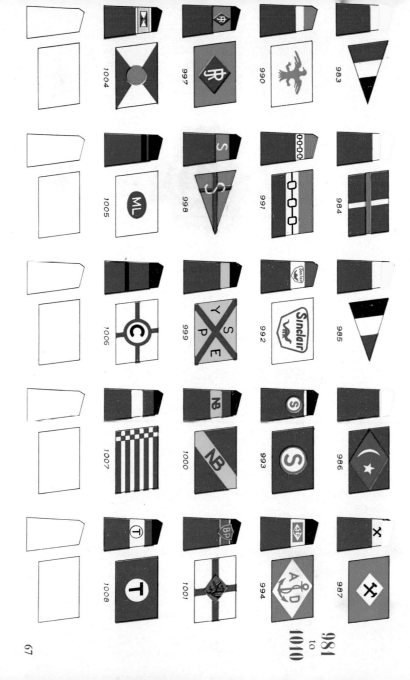

1004

997

990

983

1005

998

991

984

1006

999

992

985

1007

1000

993

986

1008

1001

994

987

981
to
1010

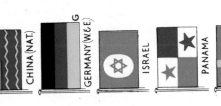
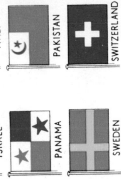

Flags illustrated: ARGENTINE, CHINA (REP.), GHANA, ITALY, PAKISTAN, SWITZERLAND, CHINA (NAT.), GERMANY (W & E), ISRAEL, PANAMA, SWEDEN

MERCHANT FLAGS OF VARIOUS NATIONS

ABBREVIATIONS. The abbreviations, used on the previous pages, to indicate the country to which a company belongs, are listed below. The numbers in **heavy type** indicate the number of ships registered in that country, the other numbers are in 1,000s of tons gross. (Lloyds' Register Statistics 1962.)

Abbr.	Country	Ships	Tons (1,000s)
A.	AUSTRALIA	299	574
Ar.	ARGENTINA	332	1,262
Be.	BERMUDA	—	—
Bm.	BURMA	—	—
Bl.	BELGIUM	205	745
Bz.	BRAZIL	430	1,204
C.	CANADA*	718	529
Ce.	CEYLON	—	—
Ch.	CHILE	103	258
Ci(N)	CHINA NAT.	102	486
Ci(R)	CHINA REP.	219	522
Co.	COLOMBIA	37	116
Dk.	DENMARK	873	2,399
Ei.	REP. OF IRELAND	82	168
Eg.	EGYPT (U.A.R.)	106	237
Fi.	FINLAND	379	878
Fr.	FRANCE	1,462	5,162
Gm(E)	GERMANY EAST	114	315
Gm(W)	GERMANY WEST	2,492	4,924
G.B.	GREAT BRITAIN	5,009	21,658
Ge.	GREECE	1,168	6,537
Gh.	GHANA		
Gu.	GUATEMALA	54	113
Ho.	HONDURAS	179	711
H.K.	HONG KONG	331	335
Ia.	INDONESIA	191	112
Ic.	ICELAND	278	1,012
I.	INDIA	72	364
Is.	ISRAEL	1,378	5,412
Iy.	ITALY	4,372	8,870
Jp.	JAPAN		
Ko.	KOREA	164	752
Le.	LEBANON	853	10,573
Lb.	LIBERIA		
Md.I	MALDIVE ISLANDS	—	—
Mx.	MEXICO	79	201
Nd.	NETHERLANDS (HOLLAND)	1,907	5,166
Ng.	NIGERIA	—	—
Ni.	NICARAGUA	—	—
Nr.	NORWAY	2,725	12,511
N.Z.	NEW ZEALAND	152	241
P.	PAKISTAN	86	313
Pa.	PANAMA	592	3,851
Po.	POLAND	350	867
Pp.	PHILIPPINE ISLANDS	149	366
Pg.	PORTUGAL	339	667
Pu.	PERU	56	131
S.A.	SOUTH AFRICA	143	237
Sp.	SPAIN	1,575	1,995
Sw.	SWEDEN	1,233	4,167
Sz.	SWITZERLAND	33	187
Th.	THAILAND		
Tk.	TURKEY	297	729
U.S.A.	UNITED STATES OF AMERICA*	3,383	21,015
U.S.S.R.	UNION OF SOVIET SOCIALIST REPUBLICS	1,313	4,684
Uy.	URUGUAY	85	328
Ve.	VENEZUELA	272	946
Yu.	YUGOSLAVIA		

*Excluding Great Lakes.

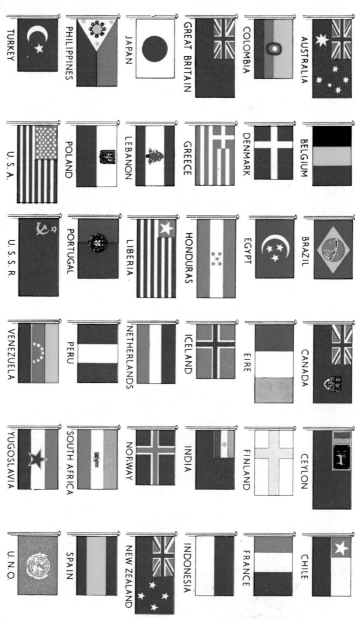

TURKEY
PHILIPPINES
JAPAN
GREAT BRITAIN
COLOMBIA
AUSTRALIA

U.S.A.
POLAND
LEBANON
GREECE
DENMARK
BELGIUM

U.S.S.R.
PORTUGAL
LIBERIA
HONDURAS
EGYPT
BRAZIL

VENEZUELA
PERU
NETHERLANDS
ICELAND
EIRE
CANADA

YUGOSLAVIA
SOUTH AFRICA
NORWAY
INDIA
FINLAND
CEYLON

U.N.O.
SPAIN
NEW ZEALAND
INDONESIA
FRANCE
CHILE

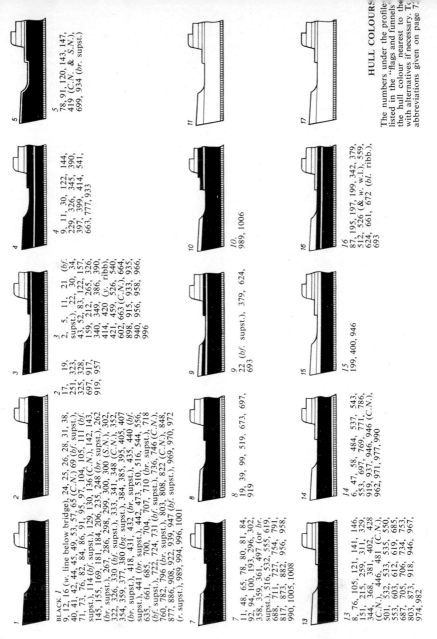

5
78, 91, 120, 143, 147, 229, 326, 345, 390, 419 (*C.N.* & *S.N.*), 699, 934 (*br.* supst.)

4
9, 11, 30, 122, 144, 397, 399, 414, 541, 663, 777, 933

3
2, 5, 11, 21 (*bf.* supst.), 22, 30, 34, 43, 52, 83, 122, 157, 159, 212, 265, 326, 340, 349, 386, 390, 414, 420 (*v.* ribb), 421, 459, 526, 540, 602, 663 (*C.N.*), 664, 898, 915, 933, 935, 940, 956, 958, 966, 996

2
17, 19, 251, 323, 325, 328, 697, 917, 919, 957

BLACK
1
9, 12, 16 (*w.* line below bridge), 24, 25, 26, 28, 31, 38, 40, 41, 42, 44, 45, 49, 53, 57, 65 (*C.N.*) 69 (*bf.* supst.), 71, 73, 76, 82, 84, 86, 91, 95, 97, 104, 105, 111 (*bf.* supst.), 114 (*bf.* supst.), 129, 130, 136 (*C.N.*), 142, 143, 145, 155, 169, 181, 184, 206, 235, 248 (*br.* supst.), 262 (*br.* supst.), 267, 286, 298, 299, 300, 300 (*S.N.*), 302, 322, 326, 330 (*bf.* supst.), 333, 341, 348 (*C.N.*), 352, 354, 359, 377, 380 (*bg.* supst.), 384, 385, 395, 405, 407 (*br.* supst.), 418, 431, 432 (*br.* supst.), 435, 440 (*bf.* supst.), 441 (*br.* supst.), 442, 473, 510, 516, 544, 556, 635, 661, 685, 700, 704, 707, 710 (*br.* supst.), 718 (*bf.* supst.), 722, 724, 731 (*bf.* supst.), 736, 746 (*C.N.*), 760, 782, 796 (*br.* supst.), 803, 808, 822 (*C.N.*), 848, 877, 886, 908, 922, 939, 947 (*bf.* supst.), 969, 970, 972 (*r.* supst.), 989, 994, 996, 1001

11

10
10,
989, 1006

9
22 (*bf.* supst.), 379, 624, 693

8
19, 39, 99, 519, 673, 697, 919

7
11, 48, 65, 78, 80, 81, 84, 92, 94, 100, 193, 296, 302, 358, 359, 361, 497 (or *br.* supst.), 516, 532, 555, 619, 688, 711, 727, 754, 791, 817, 873, 882, 956, 958, 990, 1005, 1008

17

16
16
87, 195, 197, 199, 342, 379, 512, 526 (& *w.* w.l.), 559, 624, 661, 672 (*bl.* ribb.), 693

15
15
199, 400, 946

14
6, 47, 58, 484, 537, 543, 553, 697, 769, 771, 786, 919, 937, 946, 946 (*C.N.*), 962, 971, 977, 990

13
8, 76, 105, 121, 141, 146, 151, 215, 259, 311, 329, 344, 368, 381, 402, 428 (*C.N.*), 446, 481 (*C.N.*), 501, 532, 533, 535, 550, 553, 603, 612, 619, 685, 687, 705, 706, 734, 753, 803, 873, 882, 918, 946, 967, 974, 982

HULL COLOURS

The numbers under the profiles listed in the "flags and funnels the hull colour nearest to the with alternatives if necessary. To abbreviations given on page 7

70

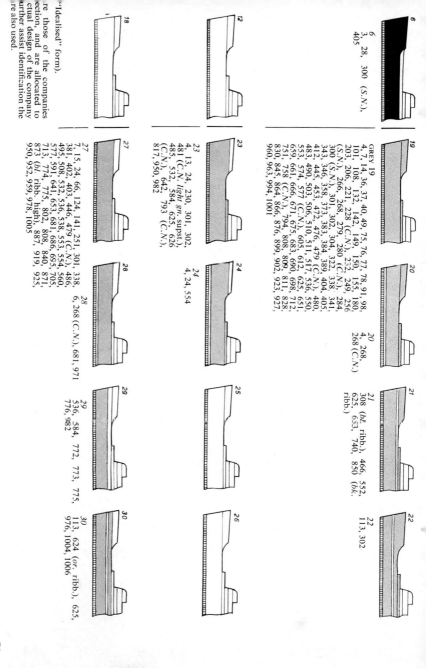

"idealised" form).
re those of the companies
ection, and are allocated to
ctual design of the company
urther assist identification the
re also used.

6
3, 28, 300 (S.N.), 405

GREY 19
19
4, 7, 14, 36, 37, 40, 49, 75, 76, 77, 78, 91, 98, 101, 108, 132, 142, 149, 150, 155, 180, 203, 206, 221, 228 (C.N.), 232, 249, 256 (S.N.), 266, 268, 279, 280 (C.N.), 284, 300 (S.N.), 301, 302, 304, 322, 338, 341, 343, 346, 358, 373, 383, 384, 389, 404, 405, 412, 445, 453, 472, 476, 479 (C.N.), 480, 483, 490, 503, 506, 510, 511, 517, 536, 550, 553, 574, 577 (C.N.), 605, 612, 625, 651, 659, 661, 666, 671, 675, 683, 690, 698, 712, 751, 758 (C.N.), 794, 808, 809, 811, 828, 830, 845, 864, 866, 876, 899, 902, 923, 927, 960, 963, 994, 1001

20
4, 268 (C.N.)

21
308 (bl. ribb.), 466, 552, 625, 653, 740, 850 (bk. ribb.)

22
113, 302

23
4, 13, 24, 230, 301, 302, 481 (C.N. light grn. supst.), 485, 532, 584, 625, 626 (C.N.), 642, 793 (C.N.), 817, 950, 982

24
4, 24, 554

27
7, 15, 24, 66, 124, 141, 251, 301, 338, 381, 402, 403, 446, 479 (C.N.), 486, 495, 508, 532, 536, 538, 553, 554, 560, 577, 591, 641, 653, 681, 686, 695, 705, 713, 774, 775, 802, 808, 840, 871, 873 (bl. ribb. high), 887, 919, 925, 950, 952, 959, 978, 1005

28
6, 268 (C.N.), 681, 971

29
536, 584, 772, 773, 775, 776, 882

30
113, 624 (or. ribb.), 625, 976, 1004, 1006

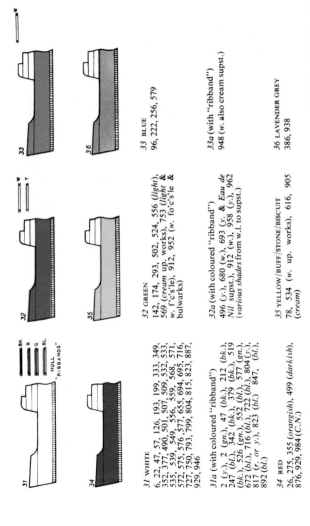

31 WHITE

6, 22, 47, 57, 126, 193, 199, 333, 349, 352, 377, 490, 501, 507, 509, 532, 533, 535, 539, 549, 556, 559, 568, 571, 572, 575, 576, 577, 655, 694, 695, 716, 727, 750, 793, 799, 804, 815, 823, 887, 929, 946

31a (with coloured "ribband")

2 (*v.*), 2 (*gn.*), 47 (*bk.*), 212 (*bk.*), 247 (*bl.*), 342 (*bk.*), 379 (*bk.*), 519 (*bk.*), 526 (*gn.*), 552 (*bl.*), 577 (*gn.*), 672 (*bl.*), 716 (*bl.*), 722 (*bl.*), 804 (*y.*), 817 (*r. or y.*), 823 (*bl.*) 847, (*bl.*), 892 (*bl.*)

34 RED

26, 275, 355 (*orangish*), 499 (*darkish*), 876, 929, 984 (*C.N.*)

32 GREEN

142, 174, 293, 502, 524, 556 (*light*), 569 (*cream up. works*), 753 (*light & w. f'c's'le*), 912, 952 (*w. fo'c's'le & bulwarks*)

32a (with coloured "ribband")

496 (*v.*), 680 (*w.*), 693 (*y. & Eau de Nil* supst.), 912 (*w.*), 958 (*v.*), 962 (*various shades from w.l. to supst.*)

35 YELLOW/BUFF/STONE/BISCUIT

78, 534 (*w. up. works*), 616, 905 (*cream*)

33 BLUE

96, 222, 256, 579

33a (with "ribband")

948 (*w.* also cream supst.)

36 LAVENDER GREY

386, 938

Abbreviations used with hull colours: *C.N.* company's name on ship's side. *S.N.* ship's name on ship's side. *ribb.* "ribband" or horizontal line. *supst.* superstructure. *up.* works upper works. *w.l.* waterline.

Colours: *bf.* buff. *bk.* black. *bl.* blue. *br.* brown. *gn.* green. *gy.* grey. *or.* orange. *r.* red. *w.* white. *y.* yellow.

The hull colours shown on the previous pages are for the principal shipping companies included in the flag and funnel section.

Generally, shipping companies have a standard hull colour scheme of their own which is common to most of their ships; but owing to the variations in the shape and construction of ships, the colour scheme for one ship may not appear, on first sight, to be the same as another. For instance, if a particular company's colour scheme is a white foc's'le with black for the bulwarks and the rest of the hull, then a ship not having a foc's'le could not comply with the scheme; however it is possible that, as a gesture to conformity, the spirket plate (or bow bulwark), if there are no bulwarks elsewhere, might be painted white.

Another feature to note when observing hull colours is the position of the white "ribband", i.e., whether it is high or low; the position may *apparently* vary between ships of the same company, owing to constructional features. The colour of the bulwarks is a feature not to be overlooked either, as the bulwarks are sometimes the colour of the hull and sometimes that of the upperworks or superstructure; indeed many ships do not even have them except in the bow. Also it should be remembered that liner companies often repaint their ships different colours if they are on cruising voyages, or operating on a different lines of run.

The three pages of colour scheme profiles are of "idealized" form; the foc's'le, without a spirket plate, is shown as one deck high, and the bulwarks on the upper deck as about three feet. Although illustrated, no attempt has been made to show the colour of the waterlines or boot-topping because the combination of these various colours together with the main hull colours is too complex, and in any case if a cargo vessel is fully laden the waterline is not easily seen. Nevertheless for certain companies who do not use the more conventional reds or greens, the boot-topping is quite a distinguishing feature; as an example Buries Markes and their associated French company Louis Dreyfus have the unusual colour of white.

In brief, detailed classification of ships' hull colours is not possible because of endless variations. Notwithstanding this, the broad categories shown here do help identification. The diagram (on p. 74) of different ship profiles shows how a standard colour scheme of "white foc's'le, black bulwarks and black hull, with a white 'ribband' at upperdeck level" might appear on each ship; the colour scheme for all these hull shapes would be classified as number 9 (although the passenger liner might be included as belonging to number 16 as well).

To show, in a few pages, all the minor variations in colour schemes was impossible. Therefore, apart from showing the obvious differences in colour (e.g. black, grey, white, green, red and blue), the black and grey hulls were each divided into three broad categories; namely those schemes with:

1. Hull, foc's'le and bulwarks all of one colour (black or grey).
2. Hull and bulwarks of one colour (black or grey) but foc's'le white; in which case the white foc's'le did not usually extend for its full depth, but started

one strake up, i.e. the height of the black or grey bulwark.

3. Foc's'le and bulwark white with hull only black or grey.

These three variations which are shown respectively as the top, middle, and bottom rows, have each been varied by a "ribband" or horizontal line. Where necessary other features have been noted against the company's number beneath the profiles; also alternative profile numbers are sometimes given to a company if it helps identification.

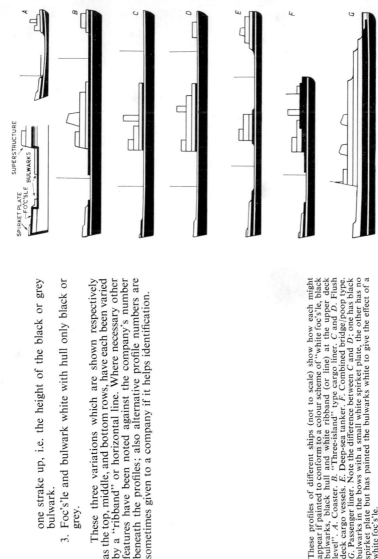

These profiles of different ships (not to scale) show how each might appear if painted to conform to a colour scheme of "white foc's'le, black bulwarks, black hull and white ribband (or line) at the upper deck level". A. Coaster. B. "Three-island" type cargo liner. C and D. Flush deck cargo vessels. E. Deep-sea tanker. F. Combined bridge/poop type. G. Passenger liner. Note the difference between C and D; one has black bulwarks in the bows with a small white spirket plate, the other has no spirket plate but has painted the bulwarks white to give the effect of a white foc's'le.

HULL COLOURS—COMPANY INDEX

The upright **bold** numbers are those of the companies listed on the pages of flags and funnels, the *italic numbers* are those of the "idealized" hull colour profiles. As can be seen many companies have more than one colour scheme; alternative colour schemes are also given if it is thought that, because of variations in ships' profiles, it will assist identification.

2 *3 31a*
3 *6*
4 *1 3 19 20*
5 *23 24*
6 *14 28 31*
7 *19 27*
8 *13*
9 *14*
11 *3 47*
12 *1*
13 *23*
14 *19*
15 *27*
16 *1*
17 *2*
19 *28*
21 *3*
22 *39 31*
24 *1 23 24 27*
25 *1*
26 *1 34*
28 *1 6*
30 *34*
31 *1*
34 *3*
36 *19*
37 *19*
38 *1*
39 *8*
40 *19*
41 *1*
42 *1*
43 *3*
44 *1*
45 *1*

47 *14 31 31a*
48 *19*
49 *1 19*
52 *3*
53 *1*
57 *1 31*
58 *14*
65 *19 27*
66 *27*
69 *1*
71 *1*
73 *1*
75 *19*
76 *1 3 19*
77 *19*
78 *57 19 35*
80 *7*
81 *7*
82 *1*
83 *3*
84 *17*
86 *1*
87 *16*
91 *1 5 19*
92 *7*
94 *7*
95 *1*
96 *33*
97 *1*
98 *19*
99 *8*
100 *7*
101 *19*
104 *1*
105 *1 13*

108 *19*
111 *1*
113 *22 30*
114 *1*
120 *5*
121 *13*
122 *34*
124 *2 34*
126 *31*
129 *1*
130 *1*
132 *19*
136 *1*
141 *3 27*
142 *1*
143 *19 32*
144 *4*
145 *1*
146 *13*
147 *5*
149 *19*
150 *19*
151 *13*
155 *1 19*
157 *19*
159 *3*
169 *1*
174 *32*
180 *19*
181 *1*
184 *1*
193 *7 31*
195 *16*
197 *16*
199 *15 16 31*

203 *19*
206 *1 19*
212 *3 31a*
215 *13*
221 *19*
222 *33*
228 *19*
229 *4*
230 *23*
232 *19*
235 *1*
247 *31a*
248 *1*
249 *19*
251 *227*
256 *19 33*
259 *13*
262 *1*
265 *3*
266 *19*
267 *1*
268 *19 20 28*
275 *34*
279 *19*
280 *19*
284 *19*
286 *1*
293 *32*
296 *7*
298 *1*
299 *1*
300 *1 6 19*
301 *19 23 27*
302 *17 19 22 23*
304 *19*

308 *21*
311 *13*
322 *1 19*
323 *2*
325 *2*
326 *1 3 4*
328 *28*
329 *13*
330 *1*
333 *1 31*
338 *19 27*
340 *3*
341 *1 19*
342 *16 31a*
343 *19*
344 *13*
345 *4*
346 *19*
349 *3 31*
352 *1 31*
354 *1*
355 *34*
358 *7 19*
359 *17*
361 *7*
368 *13*
373 *19*
377 *1 31*
379 *9 16 31a*
380 *1*
381 *13 27*
383 *19*
384 *1 19*
385 *1 19*
386 *3 36*

389 *19*
390 *34*
395 *4*
397 *4*
399 *4*
400 *1*
402 *1 27*
403 *1*
404 *19*
405 *1 6 19*
407 *1*
412 *19*
414 *34*
418 *1*
419 *1*
420 *1*
421 *1*
428 *1*
431 *1*
432 *1*
435 *1*
440 *1*
441 *1*
442 *1*
445 *19*
446 *1 27*
453 *1*
459 *5 16*
466 *1*
472 *19*
473 *19*
476 *19*
479 *19 27*
480 *19 23*
481 *23*

483 *19*
484 *14*
485 *23*
486 *27*
490 *19 31*
495 *27*
496 *32a*
497 *7*
499 *34*
501 *13 31*
502 *16 32*
506 *19*
507 *31*
508 *27*
509 *31*
510 *1 19*
511 *19*
516 *17*
517 *7*
519 *8 31a*
524 *32*
526 *3 16 31a*
532 *7 13 23 27*
533 *31*
534 *35*
536 *19 27 29*
537 *14 27*
538 *27*
539 *31*
540 *3*
541 *4*
543 *14*

544 *1*
549 *31*
550 *13 19*
552 *21 31a*
553 *13 14 19*
554 *24 27*
555 *7*
556 *1 31*
557 *32*
559 *31*
560 *27*
568 *19*
569 *32*
571 *31*
572 *31*
573 *19*
575 *31*
576 *31*
577 *19 27 31*
579 *33*
584 *23 29*
588 *7*
591 *27*
602 *3*
603 *13*
605 *19*
611 *19*
612 *13*
616 *35*
619 *7 13*
624 *9 16 30*
625 *19 21 23*
30

Hull Colours – Company Index

626 23	685 1 13	718 1	774 27	822 1	898 3	937 14	971 14 28
635 1	686 27	722 1 31a	775 27 29	823 31 31a	899 19	938 36	972 1
641 27	687 13	724 1	776 29	828 19	902 19	939 1	974 13
642 23	690 19	727 31	777 4	830 19	905 35	940 3	976 30
651 19	693 9 16 32a	731 1	782 1	840 27	908 1	946 13 14 15 31	977 19
653 27	694 31	734 13	791 1	845 19	912 32 32a	947 1	978 27
655 31	695 27 31	736 1	793 23 31	847 31a	915 3	948 33a	982 13 23 29
659 19	697 28 14	740 21	794 1	848 1	917 2	950 23 27	984 34
661 1 16 19	698 19	746 1	796 1	850 21	918 13	952 27 32	989 1 10
663 3 4		750 31	799 5 31	864 19	919 2 8 14 27	956 37	990 7 14
664 3	704 1	751 19		866 19	922 19	957 2	994 1 19
666 19	705 13 27	753 13 32	802 27	871 27	923 19	958 3 7 32a	996 13
671 19	706 13	754 7	803 1 13	873 7 13 27	925 27	959 27	
672 16 31a	707 1	758 19	804 31 31a	876 19 34	927 19	960 19	1001 1 19
673 8	710 1	760 1	808 1 19 27	877 1	929 31 34	962 14 32a	1004 30
675 19	711 7	769 14	809 19	882 7	933 3 4	963 19	1005 7 27
680 32a	717 19	771 14	811 19	886 1 14	934 5	967 13	1006 10 30
681 27 28	713 19	772 29	815 31	887 27 31	935 3	969 1	1008 7
682 19	716 31 31a	773 29	817 7 23 31a	892 31a		970 1	

ALPHABETICAL INDEX

Alternative Names for some Shipping Companies

Many shipping companies have alternative or abbreviated names. The following list will help identification if the "official" name given in the index is not known.

Adriatica Line	.. ..	804	Fyffes Line	.. ..	698
Allan, Black & Co.	.. ..	512	Holland-Africa Line	.. ..	296
"B.I."	.. ..	379	Holland-America Line	.. ..	624
Bergen Line	.. ..	405	Italia Line	.. ..	526
Bristol City Line	.. ..	151	Linea "C"	.. ..	716
"D.F.D.S."	.. ..	300	Nederland Line (Royal Dutch Mail)	..	705
East Asiatic Co. Ltd.	.. ..	552	Norwegian America Line	..	681
French Line	.. ..	946	Royal Interocean Lines	..	80
Finland Line	.. ..	377	Royal Netherlands Steamship Co.	..	381

Royal Rotterdam Lloyd	.. ..	4
Stag Line	.. ..	329
Swedish American Line	.. ..	571
Swedish Lloyd Line	.. ..	510
Turkish Maritime Lines	.. ..	817
Union Line	.. ..	951
United Netherlands Nav. Co.	..	296
United Steamship Co. Ltd. Copenhagen		300
Andrew Weir Shipping & Trading Co. Ltd.		688

A

Aaby's, E. B. Rederi A/S—OSLO	::	302
Aamodts Tankrederi A/S—TONSBERG	::	243
Aarstad, Sigurd S.—BERGEN	::	61
Aberdeen Coal & Shipping Co. Ltd.—ABERDEEN	::	365
Aberdeen Steam Navigation Co. Ltd.—ABERDEEN	::	648
Adams, Leo Reederei—HAMBURG	::	605
Adelaide Steamship Co. Ltd.—ADELAIDE		685
Adler, Richard, & Sohne—Argo Reederei—BREMEN		794
Administracion Nacional de Combustibles Alcohol y Portland—MONTEVIDEO		477
Adriatica, Societa per Azioni di Nav. VENICE	::	804
African Coasters (Pty.) Ltd.—DURBAN	::	944
Agna Cia Nav. S.A.—PANAMA	::	749
Ahlmann-Carlshutte K.G.—RENDSBURG		487
Ahlmark, O. F., & Co. Eftr., A/B—KARLSTAD	::	101
Ahrenkiel, Christian F.—HAMBURG	::	574

Company	Page
Alaska Steamship Co.—SEATTLE	754
Albyn Line Ltd.—SUNDERLAND	512
Alcoa S.S. Co. Inc.—NEW YORK	483
Alexander Shipping Co. Ltd.—LONDON	327
Alfino, A., & Figli—CANTANIA	943
Algeriens, Les Cargos—ROUEN	596
All America Cables & Radio Inc.—NEW YORK	551
Allan, Black & Co., Ltd.—Albyn Line, Ltd., SUNDERLAND	
Alta Italia, Navigazione S.p.A.—GENOA	512
Altos Hornos de Vizcaya, S.A.—BILBAO	884
Alva S.S. Co. Ltd.—LONDON	335
Alvarez, Naviera Angel—AVILES	559
Alvargonzalez, Naviera S.A.—GIJON	70
American Export Lines Inc.—NEW YORK	230
American Mail Line—SEATTLE	193
American Oil Co.—NEW YORK	760
American President Lines, Ltd.—SAN FRANCISCO	903
American Trading & Production Corp.—BALTIMORE	873
American Union Transport, Inc.—NEW YORK	81
Ameritalia Soc. di Nav.—TRIESTE	792
Amlie, Rich. & Co. A/S—HAUGESUND	788
Anchor Line, Ltd.—LONDON	373
Anchor Shipping & Foundry Co. Ltd.—PORT NELSON	19
Andalo, Roberto—NAPLES	494
Andersen, A. O. & Co.'s Eftf.—OSLO	814
Andersens, Herlof Rederi A/S—KRISTIANSAND S.	824
Anglo-Danubian Transport Co. Ltd.—LONDON	194
Appelqvist A/B, A. R.—STOCKHOLM	994
Arendals Dampskibsselskab—ARENDAL	130
Argo Rederei Richard Adler & Sohne—BREMEN	761
Argus S.S. Co. Inc.—MONROVIA	794
Armatoriale Sicula S.p.A.—PALERMO	567
Artazay Cia—PASAJES	398
Asahi Kaiun K.K.—TOKYO	216
Asahi Kisen K.K.—KOBE	303
Asiatic Steam Navigation Co. Ltd.—LONDON	102 / 540
Asiatique cie de Navigation, Cie.—DJIBOUTI	1010
Associated Anglo-Scandinavian Shipping Co. Ltd.—LONDON	991
Associated Humber Lines, Ltd.—HULL	797
Astur, Naviera—MADRID	51
Athel Line, Ltd.—United Molasses Co. Ltd.—LONDON	970
Atid Europe Line, Ltd.—HAIFA	743
Atlantic Refining Co.—PHILADELPHIA	169
Atlantic-Rhederei, F. & W. Joch, HAMBURG	422
Atlantic Steam Navigation Co. Ltd.—LONDON	898
Atlantiska Plovidba—DUBROVNIK	741
Atlas Levante-Linie, A. G.—BREMEN	453
Attanasio, Mario—NAPLES	906
Austasia Line Ltd.—SINGAPORE	504
Australian Coastal Shipping Commission—MELBOURNE	182
Australian-Oriental Line, Ltd.—SYDNEY	901
Australian Steamships Proprietary, Ltd.—MELBOURNE	541
Australind Steam Shipping Co. Ltd.—LONDON	499
Auxiliar Maritima S.A.—SANTANDER	786
Auxiliare de Navigation, Cie.—PARIS	118
Avenue Shipping Co. Ltd.—LONDON	458
Awanokuni Kyodo Kisen K.K.—TOKUSHIMA	980
Aznar, Naviera S.A.—BILBAO	401 / 556

B

Company	Page
B.P. Clyde Tanker Co. Ltd.—GLASGOW	924
B.P. Tanker Co. Ltd.—LONDON	1001
Bachke & Co. A/S—TRONDHEIM	834
Backer, Halfdan A/S—KRISTIANSUND	56
Baltic Trading Co. Ltd.—LONDON	156
Bamburgh Shipping Co. Ltd.—NEW-CASTLE-ON-TYNE	426
Bancks Rederi A/B, Erik—HELSINGBORG	717
Bang, Jorgen—KRISTIANSAND S.	629
Bank Line, Ltd.—LONDON	688
Barbagelata, Ditta G. M.—GENOA	474
Bartholomay, Robert—HAMBURG	609
Basse & Co.—COPENHAGEN	838

Company	Page
Bastian, Helmut—BREMEN	785
Bech, Alexander—OSLO	589
Belfast S.S. Co. Ltd.—BELFAST	940
Belge, Cie. Maritime—ANTWERP	536
Belge d'Expansion Maritime, Cie. S.A.—ANTWERP	595
Belge de Navigation Maritime Navibel, Soc.—ANTWERP	1000
Belgia, Armement, S.A.—ANTWERP	263
Belgian Fruit Lines, S.A.—ANTWERP	815
Bell, Hemsley, Ltd.—SOUTHAMPTON	732
Belships Co. Ltd. (Christen Smith)—OSLO	863
Ben Line Steamers, Ltd.—EDINBURGH	554
Bendixen, T.S.—LILLESAND	469
Berg, Odd—OSLO	42
Berg, Odd—TROMSO	762
Berg, Thorvald—Tonsberg	643
Bergens Kulkompani A/S—BERGEN	182
Bergenske Dampskibsselskab—BERGEN	405
Bergensen, Berge Sigval—OSLO	853
Bergensen, Sigval—STAVANGER	142
Bergesen d.y. & Co., Sig.—OSLO	502
Bergh & Helland—BERGEN	88
Bernuth, Lembcke Co. Inc.—NEW YORK	191
Bertorello, Febo Amedeo—GENOA	941
Bibby Line, Ltd.—LIVERPOOL	956
Bifrost, Rederi A/B (Jarl R. Trapp)—GOTHENBURG	463
Bilbaina, Naviera S.A.—BILBAO	769
Billmer, J.A., & Co. Ltd.—Stanhope Steamship Co. Ltd.—LONDON	105
Billners Rederi A/B—GOTHENBURG	470
Biornstad, Biorn, & Co.—MOSS	714
Birkeland Rederi, Sigbjorn—BERGEN	756
Bischoff, Heinrich—HAMBURG	662
Bjorge, Hjalmar—OSLO	656
Black Star Line, Ltd.—ACCRA	860
Bland Line Ltd.—GIBRALTAR	961
Bloomfield Steamship Co.—HOUSTON	930
Blue Funnel Line—LIVERPOOL	882
Blue Star Line, Ltd.—LONDON	982
Blystad, Arne—OSLO	818
Boe & Co., Olaf—ARENDAL	27
Boe & Pedersen—OSLO	654
Bolten, Aug.—HAMBURG	131
Bolton Steam Shipping Co. Ltd.—LONDON	9

Bonnevie, Christian F—OSLO ... 728
Booker Line, Ltd.—LIVERPOOL ... 695
Booth Steamship Co. Ltd.—LIVERPOOL ... 76
Bore, Angf. A/B—TURKU.. ... 826
Borges Rederi A/S—TONSBERG ... 649
Borgestad, A/S—BORGESTAD ... 866
Borgne, Charles Le—PARIS ... 185
Bork, P. Shipping A/S—COPENHAGEN ... 881
Bornholm af 1866 A/S D/S—RONNE ... 336
Borregaard, A/S—SARPSBORG ... 236
Borresen, Anders—SJAASTAD-LIER ... 592
Borthen, Harry, & Co. A/S—OSLO ... 588
Bowater S.S. Co. Ltd.—LONDON ... 569
Bowring, C. T., & Co. Ltd.—LONDON ... 232
Bozzo, Giuseppe, fu Lorenzo—GENOA ... 89
Braathen, Bjorn G.—OSLO ... 907
Braathen, Ludv. G.—OSLO ... 590
Brekkes Rederi, A/S Krohn—HAUGESUND ... 755
Bristol Steam Navigation Co. Ltd.—BRISTOL ... 613
Britain S.S. Co. Ltd.—LONDON ... 15
British Channel Islands Shipping Co. Ltd.—LONDON ... 782
British & Continental Steamship Co. Ltd.—LIVERPOOL ... 497
British India Steam Navigation Co. Ltd.—LONDON ... 379
British Oil Shipping Co. Ltd.—LONDON ... 423
British Phosphate Commissioners—MELBOURNE ... 713
British Railways Board (late B.T.C.)—LONDON ... 711
Brocklebank, T. & J., Ltd.—LIVERPOOL ... 421
Brodarsko Produzece Zadar—ZADAR ... 514
Brodarstvo Produzece za Pomorski Soabracaj—HERZEGNOVI ... 657
Brodin, Erik O.—STOCKHOLM ... 669
Broer, Gebr., N.V.—DORDRECHT ... 245
Broken Hill Proprietary Co. Ltd.—MELBOURNE ... 395
Brovig, Th.—FARSUND ... 591
Brown, P. Jun. & Co.—COPENHAGEN ... 343
Brunkman, Ragnar—HELSINGBORG ... 505
Brussels Steamship Co. Ltd.—LONDON ... 854
Bruusgaard Kiosterud & Co.—DRAMMEN ... 459
Bruusgaard, Sigurd—DRAMMEN ... 210

Bugge, Iver—LARVIK ... 315
Bugsier Reederei und Bergungs A. G.—HAMBURG ... 97
Buries, Markes, Ltd.—LONDON ... 192
Burke Ltd., John—BRISBANE ... 915
Burma Shipping Board, Union of—RANGOON ... 332
Burmah Oil Co. (Tankers) Ltd.—LONDON ... 508
Burnett Steamship Co. Ltd.—NEWCASTLE-ON-TYNE ... 235
Burns & Laird Lines, Ltd.—GLASGOW ... 996
Burns, Philip & Co. Ltd.—SYDNEY ... 212
Busck, Cie. Nouvelle de Navigation—MARSEILLES ... 241

C

Cable & Wireless Ltd.—LONDON ... 542
Caennaise, Soc. Navale—CAEN ... 352
Calmar S.S. Corpn.—NEW YORK ... 267
Cameli, Carlo—GENOA ... 522
Campanella Soc. Nav., Tito—GENOA ... 810
Campos y Cia., Clemente—BILBAO ... 82
Canada Steamship Lines, Ltd.—MONTREAL ... 984
Canadian Pacific Steamships, Ltd.—LIVERPOOL ... 577
Canale di Pietro, Emilio—ROME ... 172
Canterbury Steam Shipping Co. Ltd.—CHRISTCHURCH ... 544
Capano, Raffaele—NAPLES ... 885
Cargos Algeriens, Les—ROUEN ... 596
Cathay Shipping Co. Ltd.—SINGAPORE ... 562
Central Electricity Generating Board—LONDON ... 934
Central Gulf Steamship Corporation—NEW ORLEANS ... 841
Chapman & Willan, Ltd.—NEWCASTLE-ON-TYNE ... 389
Chargeurs Reunis, Cie. Maritime—PARIS ... 619
Charlton S.S. Co. Ltd.—LONDON ... 791
Charrington Gardner Locket (London), Ltd.—LONDON ... 787
Chilena de Navegacion Interoceanica, Cia.—VALPARAISO ... 1002

Chilena del Pacifico, Naviera S.A.—VALPARAISO ... 874
Chimigas Marittima Cia. di Nav.—PALERMO ... 515
China Merchants Steam Navigation Co. Ltd.—TAIPEH ... 25
China Navigation Co. Ltd.—LONDON ... 2
China Pacific Navigation Co. Ltd.—HONG KONG ... 10
China Union Lines Ltd.—TAIPEH ... 807
Chine Shipping Co. Ltd. (Anglo-Danubian Transport Co. Ltd.)—LONDON ... 994
Chowgule Steamships (Bahamas) Ltd.—NASSAU ... 897
Christensen, Ivar An.—OSLO ... 304
Christensen, Jacob—BERGEN ... 692
Christensen, T. C., & Co.—COPENHAGEN ... 891
Christophersen, H. W.—FLENSBURG ... 645
Cia. Anon. Venezolana de Navegacion—CARACAS ... 671
Cia Armatoriale Italiana—VENICE ... 928
Cia. Arrendataria del Monopolio de Petroleos S.A.—MADRID ... 145
Cia. Chilena de Navegacion Interoceanica—VALPARAISO ... 1002
Cia Colonial de Navegação—LISBON ... 625
Cia. Espanola de Petroleos S.A.—MADRID ... 251
Cia Frutero—Valenciana de Navegacion (Cofruna)—VALENCIA ... 631
Cia Mar. del Nervion—BILBAO ... 58
Cia. Maritima—MANILA ... 117
Cia. Nacional de Navegação—LISBON ... 24
Patrimonio Nacional—RIO DE JANEIRO ... 57
Cia de Navegacao Carregadores Acoreanos—AZORES ... 495
Cia. de Nav. Giuseppe Mazzini—GENOA ... 529
Cia. Nav. Espanola S.A.—MADRID ... 257
Cia. de Navegacion Vizcaya—BILBAO ... 38
Cia. Naviera Vascongada—BILBAO ... 128
Cia. Sicula di Armamento, S.p.A.—PALERMO ... 478
Cia. Sud-Americana de Vapores—VALPARAISO ... 945
Cia. Trasatlantica Espanola—MADRID ... 6
Cia. Trasmediterranea—BARCELONA ... 655

C (continued)

Cie. Asiatique de Navigation—DJIBOUTI ... 1010
Cie. Auxiliare de Navigation—PARIS ... 458
Cie. Belge d'Expansion Maritime, S.A.—ANTWERP ... 595
Cie. Generale Transatlantique—PARIS ... 946
Cie. Maritime Belge (Lloyd Royal)—ANTWERP ... 536
Cie. Maritime des Chargeurs Reunis, S.A.—PARIS ... 619
Cie. Maritime de Transports de Goudron—PARIS ... 614
Cie. des Messageries Maritimes—PARIS ... 11
Cie. Nantaise des Chargeurs de l'Ouest—NANTES ... 460
Cie. Nationale de Navigation—PARIS ... 77
Cie. de Navigation Daher—MARSEILLES ... 217
Cie. de Navigation Denis Frères—PARIS ... 29
Cie. de Navigation Fruitière—PARIS ... 652
Cie. de Navigation Mixte—MARSEILLES ... 199
Cie. de Navigation d'Orbigny—PARIS ... 443
Cie. de Navigation Paquet—MARSEILLES ... 47
Cie. de Nav. Sud Atlantique—PARIS ... 706
Cie. Nouvelle France-Navigation—PARIS ... 795
Cie. Nouvelle de Nav. Busck—MARSEILLES ... 241
Cie. de Transports Oceaniques—PARIS ... 626
Citerna Maritime—PARIS ... 13
City Line, Ltd (Ellerman's)—GLASGOW. ... 772
Clan Line Steamers, Ltd.—GLASGOW ... 400
Clarke Steamship Co., Ltd.—QUEBEC ... 672
Clarkson, H., & Co. Ltd.—LONDON ... 358
Clausen, C.—COPENHAGEN ... 264
Clipper, Rederi A/B (Einar Hansen)—MALMO ... 849
Clyde Shipping Co., Ltd.—GLASGOW ... 8
Coast Lines, Ltd.—LIVERPOOL ... 39
Coast Steamships Ltd.—PORT ADELAIDE. ... 805
Cofruna—VALENCIA ... 631
Colombine Shipping Co.—MONROVIA ... 983
Colonial de Navegaçăo, Cia.—LISBON ... 625
Colonial Sugar Refining Co. Ltd.—SYDNEY ... 87
Comben, Longstaff & Co. Ltd.—LONDON ... 317
Commercial Cable Co. Ltd.—LONDON ... 548
Compostela, Naviera S.A.—SANTIAGO ... 239
Constantine Shipping Co. Ltd.—MIDDLESBROUGH ... 1006

Constants, Ltd.—LONDON ... 340
Coral Shipping Ltd.—LONDON ... 561
Corporacion Peruana de Vapores—CALLAO ... 462
Corrado, Soc. di Navigazione—GENOA ... 106
Cory, John, & Sons, Ltd.—CARDIFF ... 44
Cory, Wm., & Son, Ltd.—LONDON ... 146
Cosarma—PALERMO ... 478
Costa, Giacomo fu Andrea—GENOA ... 716
Cosulich, Fratelli—TRIESTE ... 1007
Counties Ship Management Co. Ltd. and London & Overseas Freighters, Ltd.—LONDON ... 673
Court Line Ltd.—LONDON ... 686
Craig, Hugh, & Co. Ltd.—BELFAST ... 798
Crawford Shipping Co. Ltd. and Medomsley Steam Shipping Co. Ltd.—LONDON ... 52
Cunard Steamship Co. Ltd.—LIVERPOOL ... 962
Currie Line, Ltd.—LEITH ... 86

D

D'Amico Fratelli—ROME ... 566
Daher, Cie. de Navigation—MARSEILLES. ... 217
Dahl, A/S Thor—SANDEFJORD ... 476
Daido Kaiun K.K.—KOBE ... 428
Dalgliesh, R. S., Ltd.—NEWCASTLE-ON-TYNE ... 886
Dani & C.—GENOA ... 107
Danielsen Rederiet, Otto—COPENHAGEN ... 909
Danske Kulkompagni A/S—COPENHAGEN ... 632
Dansk-Franske D/S, A/S Det.—COPENHAGEN ... 506
Davila, Joaquin y Cia.—VIGO ... 985
De Vries & Co.—HAMBURG ... 475
Delmas-Vieljeux, Soc. Navale—PARIS ... 894
Delta Line—NEW ORLEANS ... 808
Dene Shipping Co., Ltd.—LONDON ... 281
Denholm, J. & J., Ltd.—GLASGOW ... 978
Denis Frères, Cie. de Navigation—PARIS ... 29
Denizcilik Bankasi T.A.O.—ISTANBUL ... 817
Deppe, Armement, S.A.—ANTWERP ... 547

Detjen, Reederei Friedrich A.—HAMBURG ... 132
Deutsch. Seereederei (V.E.B.)—ROSTOCK ... 842
Djimun Navigation Co. Ltd.—LONDON ... 211
Ditlev-Simonsen & Co., Halfdan—OSLO ... 764
Djakarta Lloyd—JAVA ... 368
Dohle, Peter—HAMBURG ... 350
Dominion Shipping Co. Ltd.—SYDNEY, NOVA SCOTIA ... 330
Donaldson Line, Ltd.—GLASGOW ... 84
Donato, Giuseppe fu Lorenzo—MESSINA ... 527
Dorey & Sons Ltd., Onesimus—GUERNSEY ... 248
Drake Shipping Co. Ltd.—LONDON ... 763
Drescher, Erich—HAMBURG ... 242
Dreyfus, Louis & Cie.—PARIS ... 195
Dundee, Perth & London Shipping Co. Ltd.—DUNDEE ... 947

E

Eastern & Australian Steamship Co. Ltd.—LONDON ... 21
Elder Dempster Lines, Ltd.—LIVERPOOL. ... 532
Elders & Fyffes, Ltd.—LONDON ... 698
Ellerman & Bucknall S.S. Co. Ltd.—LONDON ... 773
Ellerman & Papayanni Lines, Ltd.—LIVERPOOL ... 775
Ellerman's City Line—GLASGOW. ... 772
Ellerman's Hall Line Ltd.—LIVERPOOL ... 774
Ellerman's Wescott & Laurence Line Ltd.—LONDON ... 776
Ellerman's Wilson Line, Ltd.—LONDON. ... 952
Ender Dampfercompagnie A. G.—EMDEN ... 375
Empresa Insulana de Nav.—LISBON ... 697
Empresa Nacional Elcano de la Marina Mercante—MADRID ... 223
Entz, Thomas, Tanker GmbH—RENDSBURG ... 971
Epiphaniades Shipping Co. Ltd., T.N.—ATHENS ... 48
Erhardt & Dekkers—ROTTERDAM ... 715
Erichsen, Leif—BERGEN ... 74
Espanola, Cia. Nav. S.A.—MADRID ... 583
Espanola de Petroleos, Cia. S.A.—MADRID ... 257
... 251

Essberger, John T.—HAMBURG ... 109
Esso Petroleum Co. Ltd.—LONDON ... 155
Etela-Suomen Laiva O/Y—HELSINKI ... 387
Euxine Shipping Co. Ltd.—LONDON ... 575
Evensen, Eiv.—OSLO ... 837
Evensen, N.,Chr.—OSLO ... 729
Everard, F. T., & Sons, Ltd.—LONDON ... 78

F

Fafalios, D. J.—CHIOS ... 258
Falkland Islands Trading Co. Ltd.—LONDON ... 963
Fanges & Pahlssons Rederier—HELSINGBORG ... 893
Farrell Lines Inc.—NEW YORK ... 771
Farsjo & Co., J. F.—OSLO ... 581
Fassio, Societa di Navigazione—GENOA. ... 530
Fearnley & Eger—OSLO ... 328
Federal Commerce & Navigation Co. Ltd.—MONTREAL ... 914
Federal Steam Navigation Co. Ltd.—LONDON ... 977
Fenno S.S. Ltd. O/Y—HELSINKI ... 269
Fernströms Rederi, A.K.—KARLSHAMN ... 861
Fierro, Federico G.—SAN ESTEBAN DE PRAVIA ... 178
Finland—Sydamerika Linjen A/B—HELSINKI ... 266
Finnlines Ltd. O/Y—HELSINKI ... 214
Finska Angfartygs A/B—HELSINKI ... 377
Firth Shipping Co. Ltd.—NEWCASTLE-ON-TYNE ... 265
Fischer-Nielsen, R.—COPENHAGEN ... 305
Fisher, James & Sons, Ltd.—BARROW-IN-FURNESS ... 777
Fisher, Jos. & Sons—NEWRY ... 440
Fisser & v. Doornum—EMDEN ... 292
Flensburger Schiffsparten-Vereinigung, A. G.—FLENSBURG ... 565
Flensburger Trampreeder GmbH—FLENSBURG ... 254
Flota Mercante Gran Centroamericana—GUATEMALA ... 488
Flota Mercante Grancolombiana S.A.—BOGOTA ... 486

Fluvial et Maritime, Soc. d'Armement—PARIS ... 295
Forenede Dampskibs–Selskab A/S—COPENHAGEN ... 300
Forenede Kulimportorer Handels-Selskab A/S—COPENHAGEN ... 391
France Fenwick, Wm. & Co. Ltd.—LONDON ... 111
France-Navigation, Cie. Nouvelle—PARIS ... 525
Fraternitas, Rederi, A/B—GOTHENBURG ... 904
Friederich, Reederei Eugen—BREMEN ... 133
Frigga, A. G.—HAMBURG ... 393
Fritzen & Sohn, Johs.—EMDEN ... 180
Frutero-Valenciana de Navegacion, Cia.—VALENCIA ... 631
Fruitiere, Cie. de Navigation—PARIS ... 652
Furness, Withy & Co. Ltd.—LONDON ... 402

G

Gaard, Einar M.—HAUGESUND ... 394
Garcia, Francisco, S.A.—SANTANDER ... 436
Gardner, J. & A., & Co. Ltd.—GLASGOW ... 95
Garibaldi, Soc. Co-Operativa di Navigazione—GENOA ... 973
Gavarone, Giovanni—GENOA ... 964
Gehrckens, H. M.—HAMBURG ... 703
Gem Line Ltd.—GLASGOW ... 16
General Shipping Co. Inc.—MANILA ... 875
General Steam Navigation Co. Ltd.—LONDON ... 83
Gennari fu Torquato, Ubaldo—PESARO. ... 171
Geral de Comercio, Industria e Transportes, Soc.—LISBON ... 202
Gerance et d'Armement, Soc. Anon.—PARIS ... 612
Gerrard, Johan—KRISTIANSAND S. ... 597
Gestioni Esercizio Navi Sicilia—PALERMO ... 880
Gibbs & Co.—NEWPORT ... 965
Gibson, Geo., & Co. Ltd.—LEITH ... 69
Gill-Johannessen & Co., L.—OSLO ... 660
Gjerpen, Hans, & Co.—OSLO ... 439
Glassel & Co.—BREMEN ... 168
Glen & Co. Ltd.—GLASGOW ... 949
Glen Line, Ltd.—LONDON ... 939

Godager & Co., Bucha—OSLO ... 409
Godager & Co., Odd—OSLO ... 134
Gogstad, C. T., & Co.—OSLO ... 598
Gorthons Rederier—HELSINGBORG ... 511
Gotland Angfartygsaktiebolaget—VISBY ... 306
Goudron, Cie. Maritime de Transports—PARIS ... 614
Grace Line Inc.—NEW YORK ... 919
Graf-Wang & Evjen—OSLO ... 745
Graig Shipping Co. Ltd.—CARDIFF ... 524
Gran Centroamericana, Flota Mercante—GUATEMALA ... 488
Grancolombiana, Flota Mercante S.A.—BOGOTA ... 486
Grammerstorf, Karl—KIEL ... 347
Grangesberg-Oxelosund Trafik A/B—STOCKHOLM ... 249
Great Yarmouth Shipping Co. Ltd.—GREAT YARMOUTH ... 699
Greek South American Line Shipping Co. S.A.—PIRAEUS ... 557
Gribel, Rud. Christ.—LUBECK ... 310
Grimaldi Fratelli—NAPLES ... 865
Gross, O., & Sons, Ltd.—LONDON ... 724
Gross, Karl—BREMEN ... 447
Guinea Gulf Line, Ltd.—LIVERPOOL ... 950
Guinness, Son & Co. (Dublin) Ltd., Arthur—DUBLIN ... 948
Gulf Oil Corporation—PITTSBURGH ... 864
Gulf & South American Steamship Co. Inc.—NEW ORLEANS ... 922

H

Haaland, Christian—HAUGESUND ... 600
Hachiuma Kisen K. K.—HYOGO-KEN ... 64
Hadley Shipping Co. Ltd.—LONDON ... 734
Hain Steamship Co. Ltd.—LONDON ... 30
Halal Shipping Co. Ltd.—LONDON ... 969
Halcyon Lijn N.V.—ROTTERDAM. ... 290
Haldin & Co. Ltd.—Court Line, Ltd.—LONDON ... 686
Hall Bros. S.S. Co. Ltd.—NEWCASTLE-ON-TYNE ... 1004
Hall Line, Ltd. (Ellerman's)—LIVERPOOL ... 774
Haltermann, Johann—HAMBURG ... 449

Hamburg – Amerika Linie—HAMBURG — 803
Hamburg-Atlantik Linie, GmbH—HAMBURG — 974
Hamburg-Sudamerikanische Damps.—HAMBURG — 501
Hansa, Deutsche Dampfs.,—BREMEN — 206
Hanseatische Reederei Emil Offen & Co.—HAMBURG — 356
Hansen, E. K.—COPENHAGEN — 831
Hansen, Einar—MALMÖ — 849
Hansen, Erling—KRISTIANSAND S. — 109
Hansen, Thorvald—OSLO — 719
Hansen, William—BERGEN — 742
Hansen, Carl W. Tankschiffahrt—HAMBURG — 647
Hara Shosen K. K.—OSAKA — 160
Hargreaves Coal & Shipping Ltd.—LONDON — 318
Harmstorf, A. F., & Co.—HAMBURG — 646
Harries Bros. & Co., Ltd.—SWANSEA — 731
Harrison, J. & C. Ltd.—LONDON — 113
Harrison, Thos. & Jas., Ltd.—LONDON — 215
Harrisons (Clyde) Ltd.—GLASGOW — 951
Havraise Péninsulaire de Nav., Nouvelle Cie.—PARIS — 301
Headlam & Son—WHITBY — 141
Hedwigshutte Kohlen und Kokswerke A.G.—HAMBURG — 987
Heering, Peter—COPENHAGEN — 876
Heiwa Kisen K.K.—TOKYO — 346
Hellenic Lines, Ltd.—PIRAEUS — 268
Hellesen, Svend—COPENHAGEN — 968
Helmsing & Grimm—HAMBURG — 500
Henderson, P., & Co.—GLASGOW — 17
Henriksen, Dagfin—OSLO — 601
Henriksen, Jens—RISÖR — 170
Henry, A. F., & MacGregor, Ltd.—EDINBURGH — 380
Herlofson, Sigurd & Co.—OSLO — 828
Hermans, Armement L.—ANTWERP — 307
Hess Tankship Co.—PERTH AMBOY, N.J. — 911
Heyn, G., & Sons, Ltd.—BELFAST — 65
Hill, Charles, & Sons—BRISTOL — 151
Hillegersberg N.V., Stoomb. Maats.—AMSTERDAM — 858
Hillerstrom, Otto—HELSINGBORG — 765

Hindustan S.S. Co. Ltd.—NEWCASTLE-ON-TYNE — 844
Hinode Kisen K.K.—TOKYO — 299
Hinomaru Kisen K.K.—TOKYO — 345
Hiroumi Kisen K.K.—OSAKA — 54
Ho Chiang Shipping Co. Ltd.—SINGAPORE — 563
Hoegh, Leif & Co.—OSLO — 503
Hogarth, H., & Sons, Ltd.—GLASGOW — 700
Höglund, Waldemar (Nordfart, Rederi A/B)—MARIEHAMN — 637
Hokusei Kaiun K.K.—TOKYO — 385
Hollandsche Stoomboot Maats. N.V.—AMSTERDAM — 701
Holm & Co. Ltd.—WELLINGTON, N.Z. — 916
Holm & Wonsild—COPENHAGEN — 150
Holscher's S., C., Scheepvaartbedrijf N.V.—ROTTERDAM — 633
Holt, Alfred, & Co.— Blue Funnel Line—LIVERPOOL — 882
Holter - Sorensen, B., & Co.—OSLO — 521
Holyman, W., & Sons Prpty. Ltd.—LAUNCESTON — 493
Home Lines Inc.—PANAMA — 750
Hopemount Shipping Co. Ltd.—Stott, Mann & Co.—NEWCASTLE-ON-TYNE — 730
Houlder Line, Ltd.—LONDON — 492
Houtskar, Rederi A/B—HOUTSKAR — 326
Houtvaart, N.V.—ROTTERDAM — 271
Howaldt, Bernhard—HAMBURG — 833
Huddart Parker's—MELBOURNE — 634
Hudig & Pieters' Algemeene Scheep. — 545
Hudig & Veder N.V.—ROTTERDAM — 702
Maats. N.V.—ROTTERDAM — 152
Hudson Steamship Co. Ltd.—LONDON — 871
Hull Gates Shipping Co. Ltd.—HULL — 602
Hunting & Son, Ltd.—NEWCASTLE-ON-TYNE — 418
Hvistendahl, Yngvar—TONSBERG — 644

I

Ick, Johannes—HAMBURG — 454
Iino Kaiun K.K.—TOKYO — 663
Ilva Alti Forni e Acciaierie d'Italia—GENOA — 890

Imperial Chemical Industries, Ltd.—LONDON — 895
Importadora y Exportadora de la Patagonia, Soc. Anón.—BUENOS AIRES — 999
India Steamship Co. Ltd.—CALCUTTA — 325
Indo-China St. Navigation Co. Ltd.—HONG KONG — 935
…asa Società di Navigazione—(Giovanni Gavarone)—GENOA — 964
…ternational Union Lines Ltd.—MONROVIA — 176
…nui Kisen K.K.—KOBE — 868
Invotra Invoer — en Transportonderneming—ROTTERDAM — 294
Iris, Rederi A/B—STOCKHOLM — 96
Irish Shipping Ltd.—DUBLIN — 653
Iron Mines Co. of Venezuela—WILMINGTON — 273
Irving, T. G., Ltd.—SUNDERLAND — 147
Isbrandtsen Co. Inc.—NEW YORK — 758
Islands H/F Eimskipafelag—REYKJAVIK — 520
Isle of Man Steam Packet Co. Ltd.—DOUGLAS — 957
Isthmian Lines Inc.—NEW YORK — 538
Italia Soc. per Azioni di Navigazione—GENOA — 526
Italiana, Cia. Armatoriale—VENICE — 928
Italnavi Soc. di Navigazione per Azioni—GENOA — 847
Itaya Shosen K.K.—OTARU — 298
Ivarans, Rederi, A/S (Christensen, Ivar An.)—OSLO — 304
Ivoirienne, Soc. de Nav.—ABIDJAN — 921

J

Jackson, L. A.(Shipping), Ltd.—LONDON — 187
Jacobs, John I., & Co. Ltd.—LONDON — 704
Jacomino, Gennaro—NAPLES — 270
Jadranska Linijska Plovidba—RIJEKA — 509
Jahre, Anders—SANDEFJORD — 338
Jamaica Banana Producers S.S. Co. Ltd.—KINGSTON — 902
Jansen, Ingvar—BERGEN — 783
Jebsen, M.—AABENRAA — 573

Jebsen, Paul—BERGEN : : 371
Jensen, Jorgen P.—ARENDAL : 319
Jensen & Co., L. Harboe—OSLO : 580
Joch, F. & W. – Atlantic-Rhederei—
  HAMBURG 422
Johansson, Algot—MARIEHAMN : 213
Johnson, Axel Axelson—STOCKHOLM 279
Jones, Richard W., & Co.—NEWPORT 555
Jugoslavenska Linijska Plovidba—
  RIJEKA 905
Jugoslavenska Tankerska Plovidba—
  ZADAR 679
Jugoslavensko Recno Broadarstvo—
  BEOGRAD 896
Jutlandia, D/A, A/S—COPENHAGEN 135

K

Kallstrom, Ragnar—STOCKHOLM : 154
Kansai Kisen K.K.—OSAKA : 913
Kavounides Shipping Co. Ltd.—PIRAEUS 507
Kawasaki Kisen K.K.—KOBE : 374
Kaye, Son & Co. Ltd.—LONDON : 43
Kelly, John, Ltd.—BELFAST 441
Keystone Shipping Co.—PHILADELPHIA. 848
Khedivial Mail Line, S.A.E.—ALEXANDRIA 523
Kiaer & Co. A/S., Hans—FREDRIKSTAD. 240
King Line, Ltd.—LONDON 687
Kirsten, A.—HAMBURG 3
Kjerland & Co., August—BERGEN 720
Klaveness, A. F., & Co.—LYSAKER 308
Klaveness, Torvald—OSLO 635
Kloster, Lauritz—OSLO 721
Knohr & Burchard—HAMBURG 153
Knutsen, Knut, O.A.S.—HAUGESUND 399
Koehn & Bohlmann Reederei K.G.—
  HAMBURG 434
Komrowski, Ernst Reederei—HAMBURG 452
Koninklijke Hollandsche Lloyd—AM-
  STERDAM 616
Koninklijke Java-China-Paketvaart
  Lijnen N.V.—AMSTERDAM 80
Koninklijke Nederlandsche Stoomboot
  Maats. N.V.—AMSTERDAM 381
Koninklijke Paketvaart Maats. N.V.—
  AMSTERDAM 689

Koninklijke Rotterdamsche Lloyd N.V.—
  ROTTERDAM 4
Konow, Magnus, & Co.—OSLO : 855
Korea Shipping Corporation—SEOUL 406
Kosangas A/S—ROSKILDE 639
Kotani Kisen K.K.—OSAKA 415
Kruger, Hans—HAMBURG.. 733
Kuhnle, Halfdan—BERGEN 404
Kuhnle, S. M., & Son—OSLO 207
Kvarnerska Plovidba—RIJEKA 283
Kyle Shipping Co. Ltd.—LIVERPOOL 432
Kyoei Tanker K.K.—KOBE 933
KyokuyoHogei K. K.—TOKYO 166
Kyoritsu Kisen K.K.—TOKYO 165
Kyvik, Th. Joh.—HAUGESUND 558

L

Laeisz, F.—HAMBURG : 549
Lambert Bros. Ltd.—LONDON : 144
Lamport & Holt Line, Ltd.—LIVERPOOL 899
Lange, Einar—OSLO : 181
Langfeldt, A. I., & Co.—KRISTIANSAND S. 770
Larrinaga Steamship Co. Ltd.—LIVER-
  POOL 420
Larsen, Johs—BERGEN 370
Lattmann, Wolfgang—HAMBURG 226
Lauritzen, J.—COPENHAGEN 929
Lauro, Achille—NAPLES 892
Le Borgne, Charles—PARIS 185
Leonhardt & Blumberg—HAMBURG 73
Leth & Co.—HAMBURG 767
Libera Giuliana, Navigazione S.p.A.—
  VENICE 676
Ligure di Armamento, Soc.—GENOA 759
Limerick Steamship Co. Ltd.—LIMERICK 437
Lind, Jacob—KJOPSVIK 585
Livanos, N. G.—ATHENS 879
Liverpool & North Wales Steamship Co.
  Ltd.—LIVERPOOL 531
Lloyd Brasileiro (Patrimonio Nacional)—
  RIO DE JANEIRO 498
Lloyd Royal—ANTWERP 536
Lloyd Triestino Soc. per Azioni di
  Navigazione—TRIESTE 823
Lobitos Oilfields Ltd.—LONDON : 816

Lodding, Per—OSLO 320
London & Overseas Freighters Ltd. :
  LONDON 673
London & Rochester Trading Co. Ltd. :
  ROCHESTER 355
Longobardo, Francesco—NAPLES 85
Lorentzen, Ludvig—OSLO : 604
Lubeck, Linie A. G.—LUBECK 164
Luckenbach Steamship Co. Inc.—NEW
  YORK 348
Lund, Eilert—BERGEN 586
Lundegaard & Sonner—FARSUND 115
Lundqvist Rederierna—MARIEHAMN 670
Lykes Bros. Steamship Co. Inc.—NEW
  ORLEANS 136
Lyle Shipping Co. Ltd.—GLASGOW 550

M

Mabesoone, N. V., Havenbedrijf—
  ANTWERP 205
MacAndrews & Co., Ltd.—LONDON 539
Macbrayne, David, Ltd.—GLASGOW 937
MacCullum, P., & Sons, Ltd.—GREENOCK 960
McIlwraith McEacharn Ltd.—
  MELBOURNE 932
Mackprang, C., Jr.—HAMBURG : 636
Madison Shipping Corpn.—PANAMA 188
Madrigal Shipping Co. Inc.—MANILA 942
Maersk Line—COPENHAGEN 256
Maldivian Nationals Trading Corpora-
  tion (Ceylon) Ltd.—COLOMBO : 857
Malmoil, Rederi A/B—MALMO : 851
Malvicini, Soc. G. Officine Meccaniche
  Riparazione Nav-Vapori—GENOA 137
Mamenic Line—MANAGUA 280
Manchester Liners, Ltd.—MANCHESTER 1005
Maresca, Mariano & Co.—GENOA 518
Marina Mercante Nicaraguense S.A.—
  MANAGUA 280
Marine Transport Lines Inc.—NEW YORK 872
Maritima, Cia.—MANILA 117
Maritime Nationale, Soc.—PARIS 12
Maritime Shipping & Trading Co. Ltd.—
  LONDON 309
Marsano, Andrea & Sons—GENOA 735

M (cont.)

Martin, Louis, & Cie.—PARIS ... 576
Martinolich, Marco U.—TRIESTE ... 812
Mathies Reederei, Kommandirgesellschaft—HAMBURG ... 321
Mathisen, Gerner Rederi A/S—OSLO ... 599
Matson Navigation Co.—SAN FRANCISCO ... 722
Matsuoka Kisen K.K.—KOBE ... 261
Maurel & Prom—BORDEAUX ... 32
Mayflower S.S. Corpn.—NEW YORK ... 196
Mazzini, Cia de Nav. Giuseppe—GENOA ... 529
Medomsley Steam Shipping Co. Ltd.—LONDON ... 52
Meentzen, Carl—BREMEN ... 46
Meiji Kaiun K.K.—KOBE ... 100
Melsom & Nelson—LARVIK ... 800
Mercantile, Navigazione S.p.A.—GENOA ... 850
Meridian Schiffahrtsges. m.b.H.—HAMBURG ... 32
Messageries Maritime, Cie. des Paris ... 677
Metcalf Motor Coasters, Ltd.—GRAVESEND ... 11
Metcalfe Shipping Co. Ltd.—WEST HARTLEPOOL ... 908
Meyer, P.—OSLO ... 116
Mil Tankrederi A/S—OSLO ... 480
Milligen & Co. Ltd., John—BELFAST ... 293
Mississippi Shipping Co. Inc. (Delta Line)—NEW ORLEANS ... 179
Mitchell Cotts & Co. Ltd.—LONDON ... 808
Mitsubishi Kaiun K.K.—TOKYO ... 1003
Mitsui Senpaku K.K.—TOKYO ... 157
Miyachi Kisen K.K.—KOBE ... 481
Mixte, Cie. de Navigation—MARSEILLES ... 1
Mogul Line, Ltd.—BOMBAY ... 199
Mohn, Alf Jr.—OSLO ... 342
Moller, A. P. (Maersk Line)—COPENHAGEN ... 587
Mollers' Ltd.—HONG KONG ... 256
Moltzau & Christensen—OSLO ... 20
Monks, John S., Ltd.—LIVERPOOL ... 674
Monopolio de Petroleos, Cia. Arrendataria—MADRID ... 114
Montella, Gennaro—NAPLES ... 145
Montemar Soc. Anon. Comercial y Maritima—MONTEVIDEO ... 819
Montship Lines, Ltd.—MONTREAL ... 821 ... 197

Moor Line Ltd. (Walter Runciman & Co.)—NEWCASTLE-ON-TYNE ... 122
Moore—McCormack Lines Inc.—NEW YORK ... 793
Morey, Naviera S.A.—BARCELONA ... 975
Morland, Arnt J.—ARENDAL ... 31
Mortensen, Erling A/S—OSLO ... 238
Moss, H. E., & Co's Tankers, Ltd.—LIVERPOOL ... 736
Moss Hutchison Line, Ltd.—LIVERPOOL ... 94
Mosvold, Torrey—KRISTIANSAND S. ... 659
Motortank, Rederi A/B—GOTHENBURG ... 411
Mountwood Shipping Co. Ltd.—LIVERPOOL ... 979
Mowinckels, Lugwig J., Rederi A/S—BERGEN ... 809
Muhammadi Steamship Co. Ltd.—KARACHI ... 680
Muller, Stener S.—BERGEN ... 455
Muller, Wm. H., & Co., N.V.—ROTTERDAM ... 349
Mullion & Co. Ltd.—HONG KONG ... 190

N

Nacional de Navegação, Cia.—LISBON ... 24
Nacional de Navegação Costeira, Cia.—RIO DE JANEIRO ... 57
Naesheim, Egil—HAUGESUND ... 835
Naess Shipping Co. Inc.—NEW YORK ... 322
Nakamura Kisen K.K.—KOBE ... 59
Nakano Kisen K.K.—TOKYO ... 158
Nalon, Naviera del S.A.—GIJON ... 227
Namura Kisen K.K.—OSAKA ... 50
Nantaise des Chargeurs de l'Ouest, Cie.—NANTES ... 460
National Iranian Tanker Co. (Nederland) N.V.—ROTTERDAM ... 923
Nationale d'Affretements, Soc.—PARIS ... 71
Nationale des Chemins de Fer Francais, Soc.—PARIS ... 28
Nationale de Navigation, Cie.—PARIS ... 77
Navale de l'Ouest, Soc.—PARIS ... 690
Navegacao Riograndense Ltda.—PORTO ALEGRE ... 546

Navegacao Carregadores Acoreanos, Cia. de—AZORES ... 495
Naviera Alvargonzalez S.A.—GIJON ... 230
Naviera Angel Alvarez—AVILES ... 70
Naviera Astur—MADRID ... 51
Naviera Aznar S.A.—BILBAO ... 556
Naviera Bilbaina S.A.—BILBAO ... 769
Naviera Chilena del Pacifico S.A.—VALPARAISO ... 874
Naviera Compostela S.A.—SANTIAGO ... 239
Naviera del Nalon S.A.—GIJON ... 227
Naviera Pinillos S.A.—CADIZ ... 231
Naviera Morey S.A.—BARCELONA ... 975
Naviera Vizcaina S.A.—BILBAO ... 484
Navigazione Alta Italia S.p.A.—GENOA ... 884
Navigazione Libera Giuliana S.p.A.—VENICE ... 676
Navigazione Mercantile S.p.A.—GENOA ... 850
Navigazione Triestina S.p.A.—TRIESTE ... 366
Nederland N.V. Stoomvaart Maatschappij—AMSTERDAM ... 705
Nederlandsch—Amerikaansche Stoomvaart Maats. N.V.—ROTTERDAM ... 624
Nederlandse Erts-Tankers Maats. N.V.—YSSELMONDE ... 297
Nederlandse Maats. Voor de Walvisvaart N.V.—AMSTERDAM ... 859
Nederlandse Vracht - en Tankvaart Maats. N.V.—THE HAGUE ... 367
Neptun Dampfs. Gesellschaft—BREMEN ... 425
Nerdrum Shipping, Ltd.—LONDON ... 471
Nervion, Cia. Mar. del—BILBAO ... 58
New Medway Steam Packet Co. Ltd.—ROCHESTER ... 578
New Zealand Shipping Co. Ltd.—LONDON ... 543
Newbigin S.S. Co. Ltd.—NEWCASTLE-ON-TYNE ... 140
Newry & Kilkeel S.S. Co. Ltd. (Jos. Fisher & Sons)—NEWRY ... 440
Niarchos, Stavros S.—ATHENS ... 49
Nicaraguense, Marine Mercante S.A. (Mamenic Line)—MANAGUA ... 285
Nielsen, Marius & Son—COPENHAGEN ... 140
Nigerian National Line, Ltd.—LAGOS ... 929
Nimtz, Franz L.—HAMBURG ... 224
Nippon Kisen K.K.—KOBE ... 748

Nippon Yusen Kaisha—TOKYO ... 414
Nippon Yusosen K.K.—TOKYO ... 739
Nisbet, Geo., & Co. Ltd.—GLASGOW ... 995
Nissan Kisen K.K.—TOKYO ... 228
Nissho Kisen K.K.—TOKYO ... 119
Nittetsu Kisen K.K.—TOKYO ... 388
Norddeutscher Lloyd—BREMEN ... 553
Nordenfjeldske Dampskibsselskab A/S—TRONDHEIM ... 341
Nordic, Rederi A/B—STOCKHOLM ... 198
Nordfart Rederi A/B—MARIEHAMN ... 637
Nordstrom, R., & Co.—LOVISA ... 806
Northon, Carl, Jr.—HOGANAS ... 112
Norscot Shipping Co. Ltd.—GLASGOW ... 392
Norships Ocean Carriers Ltd.—LONDON ... 620
Norske Amerikalinje A/S—OSLO ... 681
North of Scotland, Orkney & Shetland Shipping Co. Ltd.—ABERDEEN ... 537
North Thames Gas Board—LONDON ... 407
North Yorkshire Shipping Co. Ltd.—LONDON ... 26
Northern Steam Ship Co. Ltd.—AUCKLAND ... 496
Northsea Rederiet I/S—COPENHAGEN ... 468
Nourse, James, Ltd.—LONDON ... 802
Nouvelle Cie. Havraise Peninsulaire de Nav.—PARIS ... 301
Numminen, John, O/Y—HELSINKI ... 274

O

Oceaan Nederlandsche Stoomvaart Maats N.V.—AMSTERDAM ... 883
Oceana Shipping, S.A.—COIRE ... 878
Oceanic Steamship Co.—SAN FRANCISCO ... 723
Oceaniques, Cie. de Transports—PARIS ... 626
Odfjell, A/S Rederiet—BERGEN ... 752
Odland, Jacob—HAUGESUND ... 472
Oetker, Rudolf A.—HAMBURG ... 528
Offen, Emil & Co. Hanseatische Reederei—HAMBURG ... 356
Okada Shosen Kaisha—TOKYO ... 229
Okeanoporos Shipping Co., Ltd.—ATHENS ... 779
Oldenburg-Portugiesische Dampfschiffs-Rhederei—HAMBURG ... 675
Oldendorff, Egon—LUBECK ... 244

Olistim Nav. Co. Ltd.—MONROVIA ... 628
Olsen, A. C.—SANDEFJORD ... 354
Olsen Brodrene A/S—STAVANGER ... 582
Olsen & Co., Fred.—OSLO ... 584
Olsen, Kornelius—STAVANGER ... 820
Olsen, Rasmus F.—BERGEN ... 237
Olsen & Ugelstad—OSLO ... 384
Olsson, Sten A.—GOTHENBURG ... 570
Olympic Steamship Co. Inc.—SEATTLE ... 275
Onstad Shipping Co.—OSLO ... 827
Oostzee N.V., Stoomv. Maats.—AMSTER-DAM ... 856
Oranje Lijn (Maatschappij Zeetransport) NV—ROTTERDAM ... 560
Orbigny, Cie. de Navigation d'—PARIS ... 443
Ore Carriers of Liberia, Inc.—MONROVIA ... 482
Oregon Steamship Co. Ltd.—LONDON ... 918
Orient Steam Navigation Co. Ltd.—LONDON ... 534
Orion Schiffahrts-Ges. Reith & Co.—HAMBURG ... 369
Osaka Shosen Kaisha—OSAKA ... 386
Osborn & Wallis, Ltd.—BRISTOL ... 955
Ostasiatiske Kompagni A/S—COPEN-HAGEN ... 552
Overseas Tankship (U.K.) Ltd.—LONDON ... 45

P

Pacific Far East Line Inc.—SAN FRANCISCO ... 877
Pacific Steam Navigation Co.—LIVERPOOL ... 535
Pakistan Steam Navigation Co. Ltd.—CHITTAGONG ... 288
Palm Line, Ltd.—LONDON ... 927
Palomba & D'Amato—TORRE DEL GRECO ... 408
Panamanian Oriental S.S. Corpn.—PANAMA ... 433
Pappadakis, Antonios G.—ATHENS ... 621
Paquet, Cie. de Navigation—MARSEILLES ... 47
Parodi, Soc. per Azioni Emanuele V.—GENOA ... 121
Patzlaff & Zuckschwerdt G.m.b.H.—KIEL ... 33
Paulins, Rederier—TURKU ... 843
Pedersen & Sons Rederi A/S, Birger—HAUGESUND ... 836

Pedersen & Son, John P.—OSLO ... 839
Pedersens Rederi A/S, Olaf—OSLO ... 186
Peninsular & Oriental Steam Navigation Co.—LONDON ... 22
Penn Shipping Co. Inc.—NEW YORK ... 276
Peruanda de Vaproes, Corporacion—CALLAO ... 462
Peters, H.—HAMBURG ... 272
Petrofina S.A.—BRUSSELS ... 435
Petroliers, Soc. des Transports Maritimes—PARIS ... 7
Petroleo Brasileiro Petrobras—RIO DE JANEIRO ... 517
Petroleos Mexicanos—MEXICO CITY ... 456
Petromar S.R.L.—MESTRE ... 691
Philippine St. Nav. Co.—MANILA ... 606
Pinillos, Naviera S.A.—CADIZ ... 231
Pitaluga, Ditta Luigi, Vapori—GENOA ... 92
Plouvier Maritime S.A.—ANTWERP ... 200
Pocahontas S.S. Co.—SALEM ... 184
Polena, Soc. di Navigazione—GENOA ... 246
Polskie Linie Oceaniczne—GDYNIA ... 661
Pope & Talbot Inc.—NEW YORK ... 138
Port Line, Ltd.—LONDON ... 959
Porta Hamburger Reederei, GmbH—EMDEN ... 291
Portuguesa de Navios Tanques Ltda., Soc. (Soponata)—LISBON ... 926
Poseidon Schiffahrt G.m.b.H.—HAMBURG ... 429
Prebensen & Blakstad—RISOR ... 252
Prince Line, Ltd.—LONDON ... 403
Prudential Steamship Corpn.—NEW YORK ... 844
Pure Oil Co.—CHICAGO ... 870
Purvis Shipping Co. Ltd.—LONDON ... 120

Q

Queenship Navigation, Ltd.—LONDON ... 796

R

Radcliffe, Evan Thomas & Co. Ltd.—CARDIFF ... 830
Rafen & Loennechen—TONSBERG ... 79
Rasmussen, Bendt—KRISTIANSAND S. ... 607
Rasmussen, Einar—KRISTIANSAND S. ... 253

Rasmussen & Co., Johan—SANDEFJORD . . 852
Ravano, Piero—GENOA . . 363
Reckmann, J. Heinrich—HAMBURG . . 737
Red Anchor Line, Ltd.—HAMBURG . . 18
Red Funnel Steamers Ltd.—SOUTHAMP-TON . .
Red Rose Navigation Co. Ltd.—HAMILTON, BERMUDA . . 936
Regent Petroleum Tankship Co. Ltd.—LONDON . . 988
Reim, Chr. J.—PORSGRUNN . . 442
Reinecke, J. A.—HAMBURG . . 289
Reinhold, F. G.—HAMBURG . . 177
Reith & Co., Orion Schiffahrts-Ges.—HAMBURG . . 417
Reksten, Hilmar—BERGEN . . 369
Renwick, Wilton & Dobson, Ltd.—NEWCASTLE-ON-TYNE . . 221
Retzlaff, Erich—DORTMUND . . 123
Reuter, Hakon A.—KUNGSBACKA . . 448
Riboll & Spadiglieri—TRIESTS . . 840
Richardson & Co. Ltd.—HAWKES BAY, N.Z. . . 707
Rickmers Rhederei A.G.—HAMBURG . . 174
Rinde, Kjell—OSLO . . 829
Ringdal, Olav—OSLO . . 608
Riograndense, Navegacao Ltda.—PORTO ALEGRE . . 546
Risanger, Sigvald—HAUGESUND . . 372
Rix, J. R., & Sons, Ltd.—HULL . . 997
Roberts, Hugh, & Son—NEWCASTLE-ON-TYNE . . 966
Robertson, William, Shipowners, Ltd. (Gem Line Ltd.)—GLASGOW . . 16
Robinson, Joseph, & Sons (Management), Ltd.—NORTH SHIELDS . . 329
Rod, Reidar—TONSBERG . . 667
Romano, Raffaele—NAPLES . . 173
Ropner & Co. Ltd., Sir R.—DARLINGTON . . 912
Rowbotham, C., & Sons (Management), Ltd.—LONDON . . 725
Royal Mail Lines Ltd.—LONDON . . 533
Runciman, Walter & Co.—NEWCASTLE-ON-TYNE . . 122
Russ, Ernst—HAMBURG . . 110
Ruud-Pedersen, Bj.—OSLO . . 622

S

Saanum, Einar—MANDAL . . 564
Sabine Transportation Co. Inc.—PORT ARTHUR . . 972
Sagland, Ltd.—LONDON . . 201
St. Andrews Shipping Co. Ltd.—GLASGOW . . 360
Saint Line, Ltd. (Mitchell Cotts & Co. Ltd.)—LONDON . . 1003
Salen, Sven, A.B.—STOCKHOLM . . 887
Salvesen, Chr., & Co. Ltd.—LEITH . . 989
Samband Islenzkra Samvinnufelaga—REYKJAVIK . . 525
Sandnaes D/S A/S—SANDNES . . 225
Sanko Kisen K.K.—OSAKA . . 159
Sartori & Berger—HAMBURG . . 708
Schanche, S.—BERGEN . . 611
Scheepvaart en Steenkolen Maatschappij N.V.—ROTTERDAM . . 208
Schiaffino et Cie., Charles—ALGIERS . . 1009
Schieker & Co., Reederei Willy H.—HAMBURG . . 125
Schlussel Reederei—BREMEN . . 220
Schmidt Reederei, Heinrich—FLENSBURG . . 233
Schroder Reederei, Richard—HAMBURG . . 451
Schuchmann, W.—HAMBURG . . 34
Schuldt, H.—HAMBURG . . 638
Schulte, Bernhard—HAMBURG . . 285
Schulte & Bruns—HAMBURG . . 438
Scindia Steam Navigation Co. Ltd.—BOMBAY . . 234
Scinicariello, Angelo—NAPLES . . 953
Scottish Ore Carriers Ltd.—GLASGOW . . 359
Scotto, Ambrosino, Pugliese—ORAN . . 90
Scuderi, Matteo—CATANIA . . 413
Seager, W. H., & Co.—CARDIFF . . 382
Severn Shipping Co. Ltd.—BRISTOL . . 331
Seyd, Erik Frachtschiffahrt—HAMBURG . . 596
Shamrock Shipping Co. Ltd.—LARNE . . 998
Sharp S.S. Co. Ltd.—NEWCASTLE-ON-TYNE . . 378
Shaw Savill & Albion Co. Ltd.—LONDON . . 693
Sheaf S.S. Co. Ltd.—NEWCASTLE-ON-TYNE . . 259
Shell-Mex & B.P. Ltd.—LONDON . . 364

Shell Tankers, Ltd.—LONDON . . 753
Shimazu Kaiun K.K.—TOKYO . . 465
Shinnihon Kisen K.K.—TOKYO . . 479
Shipping & Coal Co. Ltd.—LONDON . . 209
Shofuku Kisen K.K.—TOKYO . . 162
Showa Yusosen K.K.—TOKYO . . 780
Sicilarma Soc. di Nav.—PALERMO . . 93
Sicilia, Gestioni Esercizio Navi—PALERMO . . 880
siciliana Servizi Marittimi, Soc.—PALERMO . . 513
Sicula di Armamento, Cia. S.p.A.—PALERMO . . 478
Sicula Armatoriale S.p.A.—PALERMO . . 398
Sicula Oceanica S.A.—PALERMO . . 888
Silvertown Services Shipping, Ltd.—LONDON . . 222
Simonsen & Astrup—OSLO . . 766
Sinclair Refining Co.—NEW YORK . . 992
Sloan, William, & Co. Ltd.—GLASGOW . . 99
Skanska, Cement A/B—MALMO . . 284
Skaugen, I. M.—OSLO . . 618
Skibsaktieselskapet Rikisins—REYKJAVIK . . 863
Skogland A/S, Valdemar—HAUGESUND . . 416
Skou, Ove—COPENHAGEN . . 247
Skouras Lines Inc.—NEW YORK . . 744
Sloman, Jr., Rob. M.—HAMBURG . . 678
Smedvig, Peder—STAVANGER . . 630
Smith, Christen—Belships Co., Ltd.—OSLO . . 738
Smith, Sir William Reardon, & Sons, Ltd.—CARDIFF . . 696
Smith's Coasters (Proprietary), Ltd.—DURBAN . . 967
Soc. Anon. Importadora y Exportadora de la Patagonia—BUENOS AIRES . . 999
Soc. Anonyme de Gerance et d'Armement—PARIS . . 612
Soc. d'Armament Fluvial et Maritime—PARIS . . 295
Soc. Belge de Navigation Maritime Navibel—ANTWERP . . 1000
Soc. Geral de Comercio, Industria e Transportes—LISBON . . 202
Soc. Ivoirienne de Nav.—ABIDJAN . . 921
Soc. Ligure di Armamento—GENOA . . 759
Soc. Maritime Nationale—PARIS . . 12
Soc. Nationale d'Affretements—PARIS . . 71

NOTES AND CORRIGENDA

222 & 917 Silvertown Services Shipping & Sugar Line. As from 1st October 1962, these two Companies are combined. The title of the two fleets is Sugar Line Ltd. Flag and Funnel No. 917 is now discontinued. Funnel is as shown for 222, and the House Flag is as 222, but without the red letters "S.S."

243 Aamodts Tankrederi are now under new management. The funnel is black with white oval and red letters "A A". House Flag is blue, with white oval and red letters "A A".

250 Vesta Maritime Corpn. Ships all sold, and the Company is not now operating.

333 U.S.S.R. Some vessels on certain defined routes have a white funnel, with red band and device.

338 Anders Jahre. All vessels have the funnel shown, with the exception of "Kronsprins Harald", which has a buff funnel with House Flag on the side—and "Jaricha" and "Jawachta", both of which have the buff funnel with House Flag, but with a narrow black top.

353 Victory Carriers Inc. New funnel adopted recently. Black, broad red band (edged with white) with narrow blue, white blue bands, and a white monogram—a small "C" within a "V"—in centre.

372 Sigvald Risanger. Funnel is now buff with blue band and white "R".

376 E. Wagenborg. It is interesting to note that this is the only House Flag known to show the funnel-marking on the flag itself.

394 Einar M. Gaard has now gone into partnership with Siguard Haavik, and their vessels now have a buff funnel with a red monogram—a small "H" within a "G".

404 Halfdan Kuhnle. Owing to a new decree that all Norwegian shipowners must register their flag and funnel design with the appropriate Government department, this owner has changed his funnel to blue with the three white bands, in order to avoid any confusion with other Norwegian owners with a similar funnel marking. House Flag not changed.

472 Jacob Odland. Some of his vessels have a black funnel with the House Flag on the side.

523 Khedivial Mail Line. This Company has been absorbed into the United Arab Maritime Co., and ceases to exist, therefore, as a separate entity.

531 Liverpool & N. Wales. Company in voluntary liquidation Nov. 1962.

543 New Zealand Shipping Co. It may be of interest to note that the actual size of the House Flag is 4 ft. 6 in., whilst the size of the pennant is 9 ft. 6 in. long by 2 ft. in the hoist.

546 Navegacao Riograndense. Some vessels now have the House Flag on the side of the funnel.

600 Christian Haaland. Funnel shown is correct for some of his vessels, whilst some of the older members of his fleet still have a black funnel, with white band and black "H". These two funnels will be discontinued as the ships are sold, and all vessels will then have a white funnel, with black top and large black "H" on the side. At the moment, therefore, there are three distinct funnels for this owner.

605 Leo Adams. The actual colour of the funnel is a very deep buff, or light brown.

663 Iino Line. Some ships black funnel with "device".

650 Sudan Navigation Co. Funnels of their vessels are now buff with the House Flag on the side—not as a band.

897 Chowgule Steamships. The flag is now a deep orange, not yellow.

917 See 222 above.

920 Transatlantic Carriers. Now Canatlantic Ltd. No. letters on house flag.

949 Glen & Co. Company is now controlled by F. T. Everard & Sons Ltd. The funnel now has the Everard House Flag (No. 78) *on the black top of the funnel*—the lower half remaining plain red. Vessels will still wear the Glen House Flag.

962 Cunard Line. Due to the design of the funnels on some of their vessels, only two thin black bands are used.